Sleep Softly, Mama

"JUST LET ME DIE," SHE HAD SAID.

A TRUE STORY

A sensitive man's reaction to his mother's
urgent, binding request results in
consequences that could not
have been foreseen.

The Dreaded Event Occurred December 6, 1985.

by

Noel Thomas Manning

AuthorHouse™
1663 Liberty Drive
Bloomington, IN 47403
www.authorhouse.com
Phone: 833-262-8899

Published by AuthorHouse 10/30/2021

ISBN: 978-1-4184-9522-0 (sc)
ISBN: 978-1-4184-9521-3 (e)

Library of Congress Control Number: 2004097197

Print information available on the last page.

For my son, Noel Thomas Manning II,
because he adored "Grandmother Eva" so.

Eva Cornelia McLawton, as she appeared in 1912, at age 17, when she was presented to society by her parents.

"That which cannot be altered — in the course of life and death — must therefore be endured."

— Eva McLawton Ellis

Eva McLawton Ellis, as she appeared in late 1983, at age 88, about two years before her death. She had already broken her hip once, a fact that she had been able to conceal.

ACKNOWLEDGEMENTS

Space and time do not allow the inclusion of all persons involved in this story and its unfolding. I have attempted, when possible, to cite the principal characters and their actions and reactions to events. Many relatives too numerous to mention were involved in Eva McLawton Ellis's life, illness, and death; many suffered along with her and the immediate family, extended family, and friends. I was away from most of what transpired, but I kept informed as well as I could through phone calls and letters — and the few times that I could visit.

While the most gruesome incidents were originally withheld from me, I was able, after much persuasion, to convince those so closely involved with my mother to tell me the truth, the whole truth, as it happened. Thus, I have described as best I can, the turmoil, the anguish, the actual torment that the whole experience caused my family, and especially how horribly it affected me, her youngest child: the one she charged so strongly with "the promise."

According to my mother's philosophy, "to go back on one's word," to break one's promise, was akin to killing. Such a strange twist of fate occurred in my fulfillment of the commitment that I had made to her: In trying to be the obedient son who never would do anything except something good for his mother, and, indeed, in trying so diligently to "keep my word" — I ended up being the one who caused her death.

That is what Aunt Margaret and Aunt Lucia (my mother's sisters) communicated so strongly to me, but which, at the time, I had no way of comprehending.

How horrible a revelation for a son who truly loved his mother beyond measure!

* * * * * * *

My sincere thanks to my associate editor, Roxanne McKnight, for her expertise and technical skills, which aided in the perfecting of my original design and formatting. I also appreciate the suggestions she made that enhanced readability, and her invaluable editorial assistance in general.

My thanks also to artist Barry Hanson for his depiction of the scene in my mother's sitting room that dreadful night, when she made me promise *to just let her die.*

— The Author

"Every joy, to be understood, must be balanced by sorrow."

— Eva McLawton Ellis

"In sweet remembrance
of a minute, an hour — a short span of time
that lingers for a while —
the memory of which
will last forever."

— From a poem
written by Sonny Ellis

CONTENTS

Book, including covers, designed by the author.

THE MOOD

OCTOBER 1985: *The room, though quite warm, seemed cold — icy cold. I sat beside her bed, wanting to be away from this scene, away from this view imposed upon me. I could not escape; there was nowhere I could go to rid myself of the inevitable. I could neither run nor walk; even my mind felt a strange paralysis.*

I, whom the others had lauded as being able to perform miracles with this now-strange woman — I, to whom they all so fondly deferred — proved as helpless as they. I did not know what to do.

Her hazel, blue-gray eyes, now red-rimmed from lack of moisture, looked into my blue ones, searching for a response to what she had just said. Then she turned her head slightly to the right to avoid my intense but unvoiced questioning, then back to me with the sense of love I had seen so often in the past, and even so recently — the expression that only Mama knew how to give.

That expression said everything without need of spoken words; but at this moment, I was in another world, apart, beyond. . . .

"Did you hear me, Sonny? Just let me die when my time comes." I tried not to listen; it was more than I could bear. I sobbed; and as I tried to speak, only a quaver came forth.

Mama reached for me; her hand found mine. "Don't, don't." It was Mama's voice, but from a thousand miles away.

She stretched out her words: "Don't — do — that. It would be — different — if I was — in any great pain, but — I'm — not. And besides, I'm — an — old — woman."

Mama would deny her discomfort to save someone else the burden; now she had resigned herself to a fate from which there seemed no withdrawal. "Just — let — me — die." I blocked the words from my consciousness; I refused to hear what I did not want to hear, what I could not bear to hear.

My thoughts were interrupted by an involuntary utterance that came from somewhere else — as though from afar — borne of sincere seriousness, yet low in volume and pitch: "Just know that I love you, Mama; and I wish I knew what to do to make everything the way it ought to be."

The hollow sounds were my own; they bounced back and forth inside my head. I sank back into my chair, but reached forward to caress her forehead and hair, and to smooth the wrinkles on the edge of the yellow, monogrammed pillowcase.

Again she turned her face toward mine, then away. She sighed and closed her eyes against the filtered light.

If there were any eloquence in suffering, my mother expressed it with utmost dignity. But at this point, I did not care about propriety or decorum; I wanted . . . I did not know what I wanted. . . .

PROLOGUE

Watching an aged parent suffer is probably one of the most difficult experiences one can go through. I know, beyond doubt, that the last year of my mother's life was the most dreadful time I can remember.

No one should underestimate the emotional and physical anguish of the suffering person, nor discount the utter helplessness that family members feel as they watch the suffering—and the dying.

Particularly disturbing is that feeling of sitting by, attempting in vain to give comfort and aid to one who, for personal reasons, has refused medical treatment.

In many instances, the application of medical therapy and its various components can relieve pain, can heal, or add months or years to one's life.

Many would contend that there is some selfishness, conscious or otherwise, on the part of the aged person who makes a choice and wants to be released from a life lacking its former quality. But surely one has the right to refuse extraneous means of prolonging life.

I am certain that my mother never intended to cause pain for her family. Instead, she was determined to save us from that trauma, though toward the end we probably suffered more than she could ever have realized or contemplated.

SLEEP SOFTLY, MAMA (or, *"Just Let Me Die"*) is a true account of my mother's last year and how her decision affected us all.

Although the names have been changed, the events and the reactions and interactions of all characters are factual and are recorded as forthrightly as I know how.

This story, I believe, is a commentary on the individual's right to refuse extraordinary means of "life prolongation," as some physicians term it. I trust that my story will help others who may be faced with a similar situation.

The story was a painful one to write, but it had to be written before I could finally lay my mother to rest. I know that my family can understand.

— The Author

"Just Let Me Die"

I COULD NOT STAND MUCH MORE of this distress. I trembled at the thought, shuddered at the realization. The time that I dreaded most had arrived.

The phone — that convenient, even necessary, mode of address and conversation for me — had now become a *weapon*: an instrument of torture. I felt afraid.

"Fear is your worst enemy," my mother had once told me. "Latch onto *hope*. It is your greatest ally against what might destroy inner peace. You must understand that misfortune, after it is over, may benefit you enormously. Do not forget that. It's like being 'tried by fire' and coming out stronger.

"Above all — and no matter what happens — hope should never be *surrendered*," she had quietly urged, during one of her telephone calls to me. "*Never give up hope!*" That call — that advice — seemed a lifetime ago, though only a year had passed since my mother had spoken those words.

The phone, that connecting device that I used to good advantage (which sometimes brought pleasure, sometimes torment) — as I had so often talked to her — now became menacing, and, at this point, totally *horrible* for me.

For a moment, I was frozen into place, unable to break free. Then, something stronger within took control, brought me back from wherever it was I had gone. I found myself moving, as I held the "weapon." Though I felt injured by it, I could not let go. The receiver was welded to my hand, to my ear. I was speaking to someone, but this time it was *not* Mama.

Rolling forward in my chair, I pressed my elbows against the desk for greater stability. My face was on fire and my mind was bursting. The voice on the other end of the line sounded familiar, yet strange. So unwelcome was this communication that I tried to shout it away.

"*A feeding tube*? No! No! She told me never to let that happen to her!" The phone trembled against my face, and I bit my bottom lip and shook my head to emphasize my disapproval.

I knew that my mother was a lot worse. I had known four weeks earlier, when I had left to come back to my job, that she would grow worse. She was hardly eating at all, and the little she would take was so unappetizing — warm coffee mixed with sugar, milk, and crushed, soft-cooked egg — anything that Dee could get her to pull through the drinking straw or take slowly by spoon.

Our housekeeper, Dee, and my oldest sister, Rebecca Ann, were doing their best to make Mama comfortable, trying so hard to make her last months restful. And my other sisters and brothers and various family members did what

Mama and Daddy (Eva McLawton Ellis and Joseph Samuel Ellis) as they appeared in early 1920, about two years after their wedding.

they could, though circumstances and unforeseen contingencies limited their help.

But I was doing nothing but waiting — one eternity after the other — not knowing what to expect, or when; but ever anxious.

* * * * * * *

Our mother was at home; she herself had insisted on that arrangement. A hospital or nursing home was out of the question. She had told us all — from Rebecca Ann down to me, her youngest — that she did not want to be hospitalized. When her "time" came, she wanted to be among family members and in familiar surroundings.

She wanted to be *at home*, with all her cherished interests and memories — where pictures of herself and our father hung on the wall among antique photographs and paintings of ancestors: parents, grandparents, great-grandparents pictured alone or as couples, with their children and other family members, and in group outings and reunions.

Among those photographs — and permanently hanging in demanding notice — were framed, genealogical diagrams; heraldic symbols, emblems, and coats of arms painted in both bright and subdued colors. These heirlooms proclaimed descent and status, notable lineage. Impressive displays, to be sure, they held much less value for our dear mother than what many might consider "ordinary" pictures of family.

But these details were nevertheless part of the scene, a part of Mama's surroundings, as were Dresden figurines, cut-glass and crystal vases, and an occasional bronze statue.

Yes, our mother wanted to be *at home*, where photographs of her six children, numerous grandchildren, and great-grandchildren sat in easy view on this table and that; and where (only because *I* had insisted) her own life-sized oil portrait held its honored place above the sitting-room mantel.

And, as odd as it seems, she wanted to be near the piano that she had played every day, though it might never again know her touch.

But it was hard to watch her lying there, wasting away, feeling constant pain, chained in a self-imposed prison, disdaining medical aid that might prolong her life. But did she not have that right — to live or to die? At ninety, she felt that her life had been rich and full; and she preferred death to an existence dictated by tubes and machines.

She had told us all, and she had made us promise: ". . . if there is any way of coming back to see you after I'm gone," she had said, as though to strike fear into our hearts, "if you do that to me, I'll certainly come back. Now, I mean it!" Our mother was neither foolish nor superstitious, but there was no mistaking her opinion nor the strength with which she expressed it. The subject of keeping one alive with machines had never appealed to her. She had made that clear.

And never was it clearer than now as I sat at my desk, while I tried to steady the phone with my left hand. I felt my body stiffen in rebuttal. "*A feeding tube*? No! No!" I repeated.

This call had come to my office in Texas from Mama's youngest sister, Margaret, and my oldest brother, Robert, in eastern North Carolina — some fifteen hundred miles away. For several months now, the receptionist in my office complex had dreaded transferring long-distance calls to me for fear of the bad news I might receive. This news *was* bad.

The doctors had said that Mama could not last much longer without the extraneous measures she had refused. The nurses who came two or three times a week (and sometimes every day) to check on her condition, along with the two doctors who made what were considered unheard-of house calls, even in a small Southern hometown like my mother's, agreed that she was not getting enough nourishment.

She was growing weaker by the day. Dee was observing this fact, too, as was Rebecca Ann. A family conference had been held regarding my mother's rapid deterioration. Almost totally dehydrated, she was slipping in and out of consciousness. All of her children had to consent.

In the doctor's office, Rebecca Ann lost her usual composure and had become hysterical. "No — no — call Sonny! I can't agree to have that done to Mama. The last thing Sonny told me before he got on the plane was not to let them put tubes in Mama or hook her up to a breathing machine!"

And, however uncaring it may have seemed to those who did not know the full story, I was not merely parroting my mother's words to me. While lying there in her weakened state, she had reminded me many times the last week of my visit — hardly more than a month ago — and had made me *understand* that she did not want to be kept alive artificially.

She had insisted that "what will be will be," and she had asserted in her firmest voice: "Now, I mean it — don't you let them do it to me. Just let me *die* when my time comes." Here, my mother was exhibiting the only fault I had ever detected in her: a willful, personal stubbornness.

* * * * * *

"Just let me die." I cried when she spoke those words. I actually broke down in front of her. I was sitting on the left side of her bed, a friendless hospital contraption that had been brought in to make it easier for Dee and the others to tend to her. I was keeping her company while Rebecca Ann was otherwise occupied.

Following a regimen that she had set for herself, Rebecca Ann was getting fresh water and some medicine for Mama, and busying herself with matters about the house. The weather was colder, she had said, and maybe Mama needed a blanket for the night, though the October evenings had been unseasonably warm. The first week in November would promise to be "more like winter," the weatherman had said.

Rebecca Ann had taken up the vigil with her customary authority. Dee had left for the night; she would go to church tomorrow, but would come back early in the morning to prepare Mama's breakfast and to bathe and dress her for the day. My youngest sister, Francine, who had been sitting with Mama and helping Dee since getting off work from her position at a textile plant in a neighboring city, had also left. Francine would come back after lunchtime tomorrow to relieve Rebecca Ann, while she bought groceries, paid bills, or took care of some personal items for Mama.

So Rebecca Ann would spend the night, as she had for several months. Retired from work, and being Mama's oldest daughter, she seemed the logical choice; and she was the

one that Mama really wanted. At sixty-five, Rebecca Ann still had hair of darkest brown (with only a few streaks of gray at the temples), which she wore in a short and curly but relaxed style. Her eyes were a startling blue, like those of our late father: ever expressive, making it impossible for her to hide her feelings.

Attractive still, though slightly overweight, she did little to enhance her appearance except to maintain her neatness of dress, which even then was casual, never showy. She was often "too busy to dress up a lot or wear much make-up" she would say. She did work hard, had always worked hard; and had grown so accustomed to "doing" that she did not know how to stop.

Her work ethic had long since been established. She would rise every day at five in the morning and go to bed at twelve midnight; she had done that all her married life, and could not stop now. She had reared five children: the eldest, Hope, being one year younger than I.

"Beck" was "smart," as all those in the neighborhood referred to her; "smart" not only in the sense of being knowledgeable, but also in the sense of being hardworking, physically active, untiring.

Rebecca Ann's organizational skills were "second to none," as was often expressed by those who knew her best. Regarding our mother's care, she knew exactly what to do and when and how to do it. So diligent was she that she had written down every important detail which the doctors and nurses prescribed, and followed each one with explicit preciseness — sometimes even to the doctors' astonishment. "Why, *you* should have been a healthcare professional," they had agreed.

Although forever busy and never one to "fuss" over herself — especially now that she was tending to Mama — Rebecca Ann was still quite pretty to me, and I would often tease her in that regard. Her natural humor was always right at the surface. She would hug me, hold me for a moment, and say: "Tsk, tsk — oh, Sonny; stop that, stop that." Then she would hasten to continue whatever she had been doing, with a smile over her shoulder.

What Rebecca Ann may have lacked in glamour was more than made up for by the inner beauty that manifested itself in all that she did. Forever pleasant in expression and manner, she was just "simply good," many would say. She would be alert to Mama's every move and sound; she would sleep in the adjoining room, with the door open, and with one foot on the floor.

Rebecca Ann was so reliable, we all depended on her; and Mama felt better when she was nearby.

Chapter 2

MY MOTHER DIDN'T REALLY MIND having her daughters help her once in a while; and all three had taken turns doing things for her, though Priscilla's own health wouldn't allow her to do as much as she would have liked. And, whenever possible, my two brothers also ran errands or did whatever Mama would let them do for her.

But that was part of the problem: There was very little that Mama would permit. She was a product of what many called "the Old School." Her philosophy was well-defined and marked by a strict code of values and conduct. Part of that philosophy involved taking care of oneself.

So, our mother was independent and self-sufficient, not out of ingratitude, but because she knew we each had our own lives to live and our own responsibilities, careers, and families to think about. And she wanted us to have that freedom. When we were engaged in doing something for her, whether on a grand or small scale, she felt that we were

denying ourselves some pleasure or time that should be spent in our own endeavors.

So thoroughly modest, as befitting ladies of her generation, Mama disdained having anyone help her with her bath, to say nothing of assisting her in the more delicate details of grooming. The suggestion alone was enough to tap a well-spring of embarrassment.

So, it was only recently that she had consented to have the housekeeper and caregiver. And finding the right one was no small task — not because Mama was difficult, but because after all the children had grown up and gotten out on their own, Mama had not wanted nor felt that she needed a maid or anyone to assist her.

Certainly, for major cleaning chores, or seasonal "ordering of the house," Mama's children (or someone in the family) had persons brought in with regularity to do whatever needed to be done. But Mama absolutely refused to have permanent, day-to-day help again — until now. The person hired for the job would have to warm up to Mama and demonstrate a kind attitude and a genuine desire to be with her. Any pretense would be readily perceived by our mother, and she would never be happy with the situation.

Mabel Claire, Mama's long-time maid of years before, who, in pampering "little Sonny," had often served me breakfast on a silver tray, had "gone on to her reward." She had been like family to Mama and to

"Little Sonny" during the time that Mabel Claire pampered him so.

— 11 —

all of us; so, Mama would not, could not, accept one of lesser quality.

But Dee measured up almost perfectly — and since she had trained as a practical nurse and had experience, plus references, in tending to the bedridden elderly — we were all pleased. Appearing a little strange to some in the family, however, Dee believed in herbal cures — especially as found in Craven County — and suggested that she might give some root-brewed teas to Mama. She also touted the medicinal effects of eating red clay, which was readily available on ditch banks no more than a mile from Mama's home.

The doctors, as well as all family members, quickly squelched Dee's ideas thereto; but other than that aspect of her type of "care," Dee found herself fairly well-accepted and appreciated. And she could be trusted, everyone thought.

The exchanges between Dee and Mama were always pleasant, as Mama constantly praised Dee for her goodness and efficiency; and Dee would call Mama "a mos' fine lady." Yet, were it not for the fact that Mama was now unable to wait on herself, she would have been hard pressed to accept even Dee.

The reason was quite simple: Until she had become bedridden, Mama herself had gladly done the cooking and most of the housework. That's the way she wanted it.

"After all," she would maintain, "I don't have that much to do, being by myself — but I want to continue to be active as long as I can — and, now, don't you children bring anyone here to help me."

But to see her so confined, so "useless," as she now expressed it, hurt us more than even she could understand.

The room, though quite warm, seemed icy cold. I sat beside her bed, wanting to be away from this scene, but I could not escape — even my mind felt a strange paralysis. "Did you hear me, Sonny?" she repeated. "Just let me *die* when my time comes." I tried not to listen; it was more than I could bear.

And, when she spoke of having gone her "last mile" and being ready "to see Joe," none of us could doubt her conviction or determination. Still, we hated to let go. As I sat by her bed that night — hardly more than a month ago — I lamented the fact that soon she probably would be leaving us.

Rebecca Ann was hurrying in and out of the room, taking care of some bedtime chores, but she could hear and see what was happening. *"Just let me die."* My mother spoke with decided purpose.

But mingled with her words, perhaps because I didn't want her to say them, were the sounds of the television. The commentator was reporting the eleven o'clock news, and though I heard him speaking, what he said meant nothing.

I was still pondering Mama's statement, looking at her thin frame outlined behind the soft silk of her pink gown, and watching her white face in the subdued light of the table lamps. "Just let me *die* when my time comes," she stressed again; and she looked up at me.

I was holding onto the bedrail with my left hand while I stroked her forehead and hair with my right. The deep, full-textured, auburn-chestnut color had turned to a varied silver, though a few wisps at the temples and the massive bun at the nape of her neck had refused to turn gray. Until she had become ill, she had brushed her hair every day to a noticeable sheen; and she had taken pride in her total appearance. I was remembering and regretting that she was no longer able to do these things for herself.

Her hazel, blue-gray eyes, now red-rimmed from lack of moisture, looked into my blue ones, searching for a response to what she had just said.

Then she turned her head slightly to the right to avoid my intense but unvoiced questioning, then back to me with the sense of love I'd seen so often in the past, and even so recently — the expression that only Mama knew how to give. That expression said everything without need of spoken words; but at this moment, I was in another world, apart, beyond.

"Did you hear me, Sonny? *Just let me die when my time comes.*" I tried not to listen; it was more than I could bear. I sobbed; and as I found my voice, the tone sounded deep, dry, foreign to my ears.

"Oh, Mama, don't talk about dying. I love you so much." I wept as I gave her a gentle hug and sank back into my chair. I still caressed her forehead and hair, and smoothed the wrinkles on the edge of the yellow, monogrammed pillowcase. I could not stop shaking.

And for all my trying, I could not avoid jarring the bed and hurting her left leg — a broken leg now swollen to three times its normal size — a broken leg that a year ago had put her to bed and which, with complications, was causing all the misery she now suffered.

I swallowed hard, but I could not hide the emotion I was experiencing. Rebecca Ann was handing me a glass of water, and as I tried again to speak, only a quaver came forth. Mama reached for me. Her hand found mine. "Don't, don't." It was Mama's voice, but from a thousand miles away. She stretched out her words: "Don't — do — that. It would be — different — if I was — in any great —pain, but — I'm — not. And besides, I'm — an — old — woman."

That was just like Mama. She would deny her own discomfort to save someone else the burden. "Don't — do

— that. I'm going — to be — all — right. You'll make — yourself — sick. Now quit!" It was as though she almost regretted her decision, not for herself, but for those of us who suffered with her. But now she had resigned herself to a fate from which there seemed no withdrawal. And surely the end would be swift.

"Just — let — me — die," she repeated. I blocked the words from my consciousness; I refused to hear what I did not want to hear, what I could not bear to hear. Thunder rolled inside my head.

My thoughts were interrupted by an involuntary utterance that came from somewhere else, past the inward storm, and as though from afar — borne of sincere seriousness, yet low in volume and pitch: "Just know that I love you, Mama; and I wish I knew what to do to make everything the way it ought to be." The hollow sounds were my own; they bounced back and forth inside my head.

I leaned back into my chair, but reached forward again to caress her forehead and hair. Once more I tried to smooth the stubborn wrinkles on the edge of the yellow pillowcase. These creases, too, resisted my earnest efforts to "make everything the way it ought to be." Again Mama turned her face toward mine, then away. She sighed and closed her eyes against the filtered light.

"I love you, Mama." I barely whispered, but she heard.

Then she took a deep breath and spoke again. "I know you love me. And I love all of my children — and you *know* I love you." She lifted the pitch when she said "know," affirming more strongly what I had surely realized from the very first time I had looked into her face. And she continued,

"I'm not really — suffering — so much. Joe was a lot worse off . . . that heart condition . . . look how long he was sick — poor thing couldn't rest night or day, no matter how much medicine . . . and twenty-eight years ago. . . ."

As if remembering his death too keenly, she glanced over at Daddy's picture, then back toward me. "I'm being looked after."

Yes, she was being looked after, just as she had looked after our father. She was being looked after, but not by *me*. I had failed. I had made a commitment to my father that I would look after Mama when he was gone. At seventeen, I had not been prepared to accept such a responsibility; and now, twenty-eight years later, I did not know how.

* * * * * * *

With Mama, as with my father, it seemed so unfair that one so kind and good, so unselfish, so everything fine and wonderful, should have to suffer this way. The six of us children shared this special bias for our mother; we nearly revered her, but without her knowledge. She would have been quick to dissuade us from such great devotion. If we mentioned her sickness, she would always say that others were worse off. Some probably were, but "they" were not our mother.

She had admitted Daddy's pain, but not her own; and when he had been so ill, she had insisted that he have the best medical care available. But it had happened to Daddy when he "was so much younger," she had explained. "And I am an old woman — an *old* woman." She stressed the word "old" as though to make certain that all of us understood the way she viewed herself.

Thus, this present choice was hers — not necessarily the physical discomfort that came her way, but the decision not to receive anything other than the most essential medical attention. All she would accept was something now and then for the pain, which, by her very nature, she would keep to herself until it became unbearable. Even then she would apologize for "being so much trouble."

If there were any eloquence in suffering, my mother expressed it with utmost dignity. But at this point, I did not care about propriety or decorum. I wanted . . . I did not know *what* I wanted.

Chapter 3

MAMA HAD REFUSED THE OPERATION that the doctors had mandated. X-rays had revealed that she had fractured her hip two times previously — times that she had almost lost her mobility, but had been able to conceal. She had very cleverly blamed rheumatism for her sudden lack of vigor but had agreed, though reluctantly, to use a walker until she became her "old self" again.

But this third break was more serious and more difficult to hide. She had crawled through four rooms, from the kitchen to the sitting room couch, and had sat there alone all night and the following day until Rebecca Ann had come on her usual nightly visit.

It was not until the next afternoon, when Rebecca Ann had found Mama sitting in the same position on the couch, that she realized something was wrong. Uncharacteristically, Mama was wearing the same housedress that she had worn two days before, and Rebecca Ann noticed an

unpleasant odor on her body, which embarrassed Mama beyond description.

Closer examination revealed a painful irritation of her backside. Mama had not told anyone; she would just wait until she was better and then tend to herself. She would go about her business and hope that no one would ever know. But, of course, she must have feared the inevitable.

Against loud protests, Rebecca Ann and Robert had taken her to the hospital emergency room. Robert had carried Mama in his arms. Her obstinacy regarding herself became evident as she raised her hand to quiet the doctor. She had said simply, but directly: "I'm too old; no one's going to cut on me — just take me home." No amount of coaxing would convince her that a pin in her hip might afford her several more years of active life. But she would compromise. She would consent now to have a housekeeper.

Still, the doctors weren't satisfied. They attempted a last resort. "Call Sonny. Have him fly home. Don't you think he could impress upon her the necessity of this operation?" Rebecca Ann and Robert didn't know whether that would work, but it was worth a try.

Mama's "baby," born when she was "nearly fifty," as many in the family would express it, had been able more than once to work miracles with his mother. But in actuality *this* decision must be hers. She was totally competent, the doctors concurred; and without her personal, signed consent, they would not — they could not — operate. But maybe Sonny could persuade her to sign.

But surely I couldn't encourage my mother to have surgery where always a degree of risk existed, even if I wanted her to have that surgery. What if something went wrong during the operation? Would I ever be able to forgive myself for talking her into doing something against her will? Didn't I already feel guilty enough for having left her alone five years before, travelling west from the East Coast to take another job — a move that had made her sorrowful? "All my children are nearby," she had said. "Why must you go?"

Didn't my heart break with every phone call and exchange of letters in which she would ask the same question: "Why don't you come on home?" Didn't I want her to be happy, comfortable, and secure? Didn't I hope that she would someday understand that "leaving" was something I had to do for myself?

Yet, I wondered, if I'd been there, could I have prevented the fall, or at least gotten her some immediate attention? Sitting for two days and nights on the couch had given her plenty of time to think through the pain and decide whether she would accept medical help. Obviously, she had decided that she would not. She had resisted doctors all of her life — not that she didn't trust them, but because she had never given in to pain or discomfort.

And she'd known about pain, the physical as well as the emotional, for she had delivered four daughters and four sons at home; and the second daughter and the first son had both died as infants. But her last delivery — my birth — had been her most difficult and had nearly cost her life.

Well into middle age, she had been too old for childbearing, the doctors said. Indeed, they thought that she had gone through menopause the year before, so the child that

she was carrying was an "oddity" to say the least. They had confided to my father that they hoped my mother would miscarry during the early months.

"This baby could be malformed or retarded," the doctors had cautioned — but Mama would not accept that possibility, though secretly she must have worried. And the pregnancy, complicated by her run-down condition, kidney problems, extremely high blood pressure, and edema, had culminated in a breach birth. She had stood that; she could stand anything.

So, this broken hip couldn't be all that bad, she had decided. To convince her otherwise was impossible. But things *were* "that bad"; they had gotten out of control. Now the doctors were talking about a feeding tube!

These and other thoughts converged in the narrow channel of my mind as I still held the phone. My thoughts were mixing with Robert's words and becoming confused, disturbing. Robert was saying something about Mama's skin. Something had happened this past Wednesday night after Dee had bathed and dressed her, and while Joseph was helping Dee and Rebecca Ann turn Mama to a better position on the bed.

An outdoorsman and four years my senior, my brother Joseph took pride in his strength; but crisis situations made him feel weak; and seeing Mama's skin tear from her flesh when they moved her had been too much for him.

Robert was outlining details I tried not to hear. At once I wanted to know everything, and nothing. I could not reconcile the dilemma.

I shifted the phone. "I can't stand for Mama to suffer.

It nearly kills me to know that she's lying there so helpless — and what you're telling me now is so terrible —"

"What do you think it does to those of us watching her, Sonny? Her sisters love her, too, you know." Aunt Margaret was speaking on the extension. She sounded rather annoyed that more wasn't being done for Mama.

Did I appear to be that poor in pity, that lacking in tenderness? Surely Aunt Margaret could not be thinking that of me.

Aunt Margaret had adored our mother since childhood, for "Eva was always kind" to her; and Aunt Margaret couldn't bear for even a kitten to suffer — let alone her sister. She made frequent visits to Mama's house, along with the other two sisters, Lucia and Leela, and Leela's son, Richard. They brought flowers for her, elegant bedgowns and matching linens, desserts, and anything they thought Mama could or would use.

The situation was grievous for my mother's sisters. Aunt Lucia would sometimes weep openly. Most often Aunt Leela kept her feelings inside and would sit quietly near my mother, while Aunt Margaret would conduct herself with her usual confidence and remain erect in posture and attitude.

A retired schoolteacher, Aunt Margaret was probably the most vocal of the sisters. It was natural for her to step in to say what she thought, and she did this in face-to-face conversations as well as on the phone.

Thus, she continued her course of reasoning with me. "Listen, Sonny, even though the tube may do nothing more than prolong her life, we have to think of what will help

your mother feel better. We can't just let her starve. If they can get some nourishment in her, maybe she'll get stronger and come out of this." And she stressed again, this time with more volume, so as to make certain that I could hear above any possible interference on the line:

"*We cannot just sit by and let Eva starve! It would be kinder to take a gun* —" Aunt Margaret stopped short of what she was about to say, and some merciful something within my consciousness blocked out her last statement. But I did hear what she again repeated: "We cannot just sit back and watch your mother *starve!*"

"I know, Aunt Margaret. None of us want that for Mama. None of us want her to be in her present state — you know that — but Mama has made it clear that she doesn't want the tube. How can we go against her wishes without later feeling some regret? I really don't know what to do — I *really* don't."

With that, I heard Robert's voice again. "So you don't think we should have the feeding tube put in?" I heard a catch in his voice. He had pleaded with Mama on more than one occasion to let him take her to the hospital for treatment, even telling her that after she had been there for a few hours he would bring her back home if she really insisted. He just wanted to get some help for her — anything to make her feel better; and he was willing to try any approach.

But always Mama had said no, though she had made ample provision over the years for any care she might need. At this point in her life, she was financially independent and could buy anything she wanted. But she had been seen to deprive herself of luxuries she could well afford, because she was content to live simply, even frugally, so that those she loved might have more. She had been more than generous to us all: a dollar here and a hundred there, or a thousand, or even ten thousand — or more. And no one knew how much she really did for others, for she was not one to tell about such matters.

Reflecting on that aspect of her character, I knew that none of us ever needed any material thing from our mother to know that she loved us. But giving was one method with which she felt especially comfortable. It made her feel good. But, I wondered, would she ever feel physically good again?

It appeared now that such was well out of reach. From where I sat, physical comfort seemed to be something that no sum of money could purchase for her, because of her resistance. It was heartbreaking. Once more the phone was shaking against my face.

Robert asked again, "What about the *tube*, Sonny?" The sound seemed amplified in my ear — too loud, too threatening. I labored over the question, knowing what Mama wanted and knowing that all of us wanted her to get better. But what was better? And what was *appropriate* for *Mama*?

That was the real question. The doctors had presented the options to Mama and to us. As long as she was competent, decisions rested with her. When she grew weaker and began to slip in and out of consciousness, *we* would have to assume the responsibility. Matters had arrived at that state now, Robert was telling me over the phone; and something had to be decided — and very soon.

"The *tube*, Sonny, what about it?" The decision weighed heavy upon me. But why must it? Whatever I said,

whatever my judgment — if the decision did indeed hinge upon my word — might make the real difference. Whichever way the decision went, I might be driving that proverbial nail. I didn't feel ready or able to handle that responsibility.

I took one of the deepest breaths in my memory before I answered: "Robert, I'll go along with whatever the others want. I just cannot say 'Do it' in view of what Mama made us promise." I swallowed the lump that was beginning to choke me. "Still, I won't go against anything the *rest* of you decide, but she did make us *promise*."

Robert held onto my words: ". . . *what Mama made us promise* — you're right, Sonny, we really can't do it — or at least I don't reckon we ought to —"

A pause, then Aunt Margaret spoke her good-byes with obvious disappointment, yet offering her usual encouragement, while Robert continued: "Do you know when you might be coming home — again?" For Robert to ask, I knew that matters were very grave.

"Do you think I should come *now*?" I wanted to hear him say no, but I expected the affirmative.

"Let me talk to the doctors. I don't want to worry you, but Mama *is* a lot worse. It might not . . . be long." Then, in a hurried effort to assure me: "We'll let you know as soon as we are told something more definite."

I hung up the receiver, feeling as though I had just closed the lid on Mama's coffin. I had to do something. I'd wire some more flowers — but I must call her doctors, too; and I must try to talk to Mama. Yesterday her voice had been hardly audible, but she had managed a few words. Maybe I could get her to say something today. Dee had said

that Mama tried especially hard to talk when I called. "She'll do anythin' fo 'ah baby." She had even eaten infant food without objection several weeks back, because Dee had told her that I'd sent it. Such a short while ago, yet an eternity.

To talk to Mama now might or might not help, and I certainly didn't want to tire her. But maybe the sound of her voice would allay my worst fears, and maybe hearing me speak would somehow strengthen her. My mind tried to reason that she would pull through this crisis.

Chapter 4

I DIALED THE NUMBER, and after several rings Dee came on the line. I hesitated too long, and Dee was about to hang up when I found my voice. ". . . How's Mama, Dee?"

"Well, Sonny, I wish I could tell yo' some' um good, but I cain't. Cain't get'a to take anythin' through the straw, and she's got a lot weakah. But I think she goin' t'feel bettah. 'Beck' has gone f'moah medicine — an' the doctah's on his way."

"Could I talk to her, Dee? Is she able to speak?"

"Let m' see. Wait while I take the phone to t'bed." I heard her speaking softly to Mama in her affectionate black dialect: "Mothah, it's y'baby. Can yo' talk to 'im?"

The whisper was unmistakenly my mother's, and her words were slurred; and then came that definite, haunting refrain: "Hello . . . baby . . . you coming home?"

What she did not say then, but what she had generally tagged on to that question, was a remark she had inherited from her own mother, and one that she had usually sung over the phone: "What is home without a 'baby'?" It did not matter that I was forty-five.

I had heard that obsessive query a million times in my mind and heart, and almost as frequently, it seemed, from my mother's lips. That question was overpower-

The author at 45, as he appeared during "that time."

ing and amplified a thousandfold each time she asked: ". . . you coming *home*?"

Something — it was her voice — jolted me back to the present. "What, Mama?" During my pondering, pensive wondering, as I had tried to push away the unpleasantness of this mood, I had not understood her clearly. "What, Mama? What?"

Gathering what energy she could, she asked again — this time with urgency: *"You coming home?"*

"I'll come as soon as I can, Mama." She was so tired. I was afraid for her to talk any longer. "As soon as I can, Mama," I repeated. "Now I'll let you go. You try to get some rest — okay? And I love you — all right?"

With great effort her words came, but with as much conviction as I'd ever heard her speak: "You . . . know . . . I love you. . . ." Her voice trailed off. It would be the last time she'd ever speak to me.

Rebecca Ann's daughter, Hope, my oldest niece, came on the line: "Sonny, Dee didn't want to tell you, but the last two days and nights have been particularly bad for Grandma. The medicine they've been giving her by mouth doesn't relieve the pain at all. In fact, it causes terrible cramps because there's no food in her stomach, and the little she has been able to swallow comes right back up.

"She's been too weak to pull anything through the straw since yesterday morning — hasn't had anything since then — hardly a sip of water, even. Dee and Mother have been giving her that with a medicine dropper. The shots the doctors give hardly even touch the pain, and they nauseate Grandma. She's been gagging a lot. And the spasms in that leg come one after the other now; and along with everything else, I just don't know —"

Hope was keying in a bad but honest picture for me. Only a year younger than I, she was more like a sister than a niece; we had been close since childhood. She had been, and was now, as good to Mama as any granddaughter could be. She strove to encourage Mama when the others seemed unable. But lately, all of her tangible goodness had been little more than useless motions. She, too, shared the overwhelming frustration that seemed to smother us all.

"I've been here since early this morning, Sonny. It's three o'clock our time — must be about two Central —" She didn't wait for my answer. "To tell you the truth, Sonny, Grandma hasn't taken even a sip of water today, and is so much weaker, as I told you. The real crisis began Wednesday night, I think, when the pain became almost unbearable — oh — I hate to be telling you this, but you ought to know.

"She actually cried out several times last night, yesterday, and the night before, and you know she must really have been suffering." She paused. "I've never heard Grandma complain even a little, let alone cry out." She cleared her throat in an effort to disguise her own emotion. Hope and I had shared a special bond since our early years, so I knew what she was feeling; and she knew that what she was telling me now was all but tearing me apart.

Chapter 5

MORE THAN A THOUSAND THUNDERS roared in my head as I attempted to quiet my thoughts: "Last night; this morning; pain; crying out; suffering." All related to my mother.

Oh God, I groaned, didn't she used to pray: "Let me go when evening's spread against the sky — when the scroll of day has met the night"?

Evening, the sky, the sunsets she'd watched from the porch — how long had it been since she'd seen a sunset from her favorite spot? At least a year.

The big porch: her favorite summertime and autumn retreat, shaded by the giant oaks that framed the large farmhouse; where she'd wait for the cotton bush to bloom in pinkish-purple, and watch for the cape jasmines and sweet betsies to blossom, and the dogwood trees and the azaleas; where the fragrance of her numerous flowers wafted through the yard on agreeable breezes; where birds and crickets sang

in harmony against the distant call of whippoorwills: contentment.

I could see the green rocker she'd sat in during peaceful twilights as she watched for an occasional frog to climb the steps and sit at her feet. Lying also by her chair, and as close as they could get to her, would be Tammy, her favorite cat, and Brandywyne, the lovable, white German shepherd, who kept constant, but unnecessary, guard.

Brave but lazy Tammy would often climb or jump onto the banister in front of Mama and fall asleep — oblivious to everything except her mistress who sat nearby. Mama, on seeing the old cat stir, would rise from her chair, gently lift the aging, striped tabby, and place her back on the hook rug beside one of the stone flowerpots — for greater comfort and safety. A thump of Brandy's tail would record his approval.

I could also see Mama, as she sat in her chair, turn her head to the left, lean forward, and watch for lightning bugs to flash signals in the distant woods. Then she'd look upward and outward toward the darkening sky and wait for the stars to appear in their various patterns, which she would enjoy for a long while before she'd go inside, wondering — sometimes aloud — if man indeed "had really walked on the moon."

The cruel, inevitable reality of the past few days had arrived all too quickly, overtaking her and all of us; and killing me with a pain that could not be touched or soothed. The past did not remain where it was supposed to stay. It would return and return and return — in disturbing remembrance. And the impending future seemed too foreboding to consider. Already it was December, the winter of Mama's life.

A sound startled me. Hope questioned my long silence. "Sonny, did you hear me?" Then she was telling me
more. "Priscilla has just left. Brought Grandma one of those
good spice cakes she bakes. Knew she wouldn't be able to
eat any of it, but just had to do something, she said. She'd
been in bed herself for several days with that inner ear
problem."

Priscilla, the second of Mama's children, and next in
age to Rebecca Ann, Hope's mother, had been ill for thirty years or more: operation upon operation, and a distinct
nervousness resulting from a near rape she had suffered
when she was sixteen; and for the past several years she
had been plagued by Meniere's disease, which affected her
equilibrium adversely.

The attacks came without warning, producing severe
pain in the ears and head, weakness, nausea, and disorien-
tation, invariably putting her to bed. But with a resolve from
somewhere deep within herself, Priscilla tried to keep house,
to look after the needs of her husband and an unmarried
daughter, and to do what she could for our mother.

"Priscilla was sort of emotional today, Sonny — which
is understandable. And Joseph took it as long as he could.
When Grandma's skin tore Wednesday night —" Hope
stopped in midsentence, as if she'd said something she hadn't
wanted to say. "Ah — he's out on the porch now, smoking
one cigarette after the other. You know how he is. Very fidg-
ety. Said the landscaping project would just have to wait.

"Aunt Margaret and the others were here just a
while ago — and Francine will be here right after work.
She'll spend the weekend. Robert went home with Aunt Margaret. During the turmoil, he misplaced your office number.

Aunt Margaret told him to call from her house. She had the number there."

"I've just talked to them."

"You mean Robert and Aunt Margaret?" I told her yes, and she continued: "Oh, then you know what they're planning — or at least what the doctors have said is necessary?"

"Yes, I know — I'm sorry, Hope, I have to go. Tell Mama that I love her."

"I will."

I fairly slammed the receiver into its cradle, then hastily dialed the long-distance operator. I gave the number for the medical center and asked to speak person-to-person to either of my mother's doctors. When connection was made, I heard the receptionist speak in excited tones to one of the nurses. "Tell Dr. Mallison that it's Sonny Ellis." Hardly a moment passed before I heard the doctor's voice.

"Hello, Sonny. You're worried about your mother, aren't you?" Knowing my personality, he didn't need to wait for my answer. "Your sister's been here, Sonny, and Dr. Jackson has just gone out there — to your mother's home. I was there yesterday afternoon and late last night. Have you had contact with any of the family today?"

I drew a deep breath, and gave him brief accounts of the conversations I'd had with Robert and Aunt Margaret and what Dee and Hope had told me. I mustered what courage I could to pose the question I needed to ask, knowing that Dr. Mallison would be truthful yet sensitive to my feelings. "How long can she last? A few weeks?"

"Oh, no, Sonny. I don't think so. Of course, we're not God, but from a medical standpoint, it can't be more than a few days at most."

Such finality. "A few *days*? Just a few *days*?"

"I'm afraid so. Your mother's skin has begun to tear — did they tell you that? She's so dehydrated — has nearly lost all body fluids, and is so weak. We asked her again — yes, Wednesday morning — the day before yesterday — about the feeding tube — about putting her in the hospital. She said no again. We expected that, but we wanted to present that possibility in case she had changed her mind. And after what happened Wednesday night, well . . .

"I'm frankly of the opinion now that very little can be done anyway — I have to be honest with you. I'm surprised that she has lasted this long. Thought she'd die of an infection or pneumonia before now, but she's been really strong — good heart and lungs. But her right carotid artery has become blocked, as well as a salivary gland, and she has been losing consciousness periodically for the past three days.

"Are you hearing me well, Sonny?" I told him yes, and he continued with deliberate exactness but also with the cordial tone he'd always used with me.

"The only thing that could possibly help now would be the feeding tube — and that would offer only prolongation. And, as you have insisted, that's clearly not what your mother wants. Yet, the family must decide now what they wish for her. Your mother is in no condition to make decisions about anything at this point. Since there is no written statement against the tube or hospitalization, and no designated power of attorney, her children — the six of you — could mandate

what you wish at this juncture."

"But, Dr. Mallison, I don't believe we should go against my mother's wishes."

"I don't blame you, Sonny. If she were my mother, I wouldn't either. But as doctors, we have to present alternatives — just in case you wish to implement them. Your mother's so very tired. I think she's ready to go." He hesitated, then affirmed: "She certainly has that right."

"I've always felt that way, Dr. Mallison, and surely I don't want to lose her — but knowing she's suffered so much — well, tell me — do you think that I should make plans to come home now?" Somehow, I hoped that my question would postpone what lay ahead.

"I can't decide for you, Sonny, but if not today, you should surely make plans soon. She can't last much longer without the tube. I'm sorry, Sonny; but I have to be honest."

I thanked him as best I could and said good-bye. A drum pounded in my head. Innumerable thoughts whirled together into a blur of "Why? Why not? No! Come home, Sonny. When *are* you coming home? Don't you let them do it to me — now, I mean it. If there's any way of coming back *... Just ... let ... me ... die."*

I grabbed my head with both hands, closing my ears against noises that came from my conscious mind. I had to leave. I could not stay at the office with everything as it was. I felt as though I were falling apart. I really needed to be at the office, but I needed to be at home, too. The earthquakes rumbling through my mind made it impossible to concentrate on work. Today being Friday, there were no pressing deadlines to be met; still, some pending items required my

attention. Certainly my assistant, Marilyn, could take my place and attend to any necessary details of the work. She could make final copy approval for publications and meet with printing representatives who were scheduled for the late afternoon.

With a hand on my shoulder, she strongly suggested that I leave, that I allow her to take charge. A longtime friend, she allowed me to share with her the situation as it unfolded back home, almost on a daily basis; and she was well aware of the inner conflict I was experiencing.

As managing editor of a private foundation, I did feel a strong obligation to the company; for that reason I had resisted taking a leave of absence to be with my family. I was beginning to question my importance and the rationale behind my decision. Surely no one was indispensable; I knew I wasn't. Why, then, was I still here?

Perhaps I was too afraid to face the gravity of my mother's illness. Work may have been an escape, a respite from the pressures of sickness and what seemed like accelerating doom. However great my responsibility at the office, I felt another, perhaps stronger, responsibility someplace else, and one which hurt more than could be explained. Of the six, I was the only child away from home. I was the one for whom she was asking. If only she would stop. If only I didn't feel so guilty. But what could I do about it all?

Tying up what loose ends I could, I left the office, entrusting the work to my capable assistant's judicious handling. I knew that she'd take care of everything, and at the same time would send good thoughts my way. Staff members aware of the trouble wished me well, and insisted that I let them know of any change. I thanked them and hastened

out the door. I had to get to my apartment. There, maybe I could pull myself together. There, maybe I could make sense out of all that was happening. There, I'd start making arrangements for the trip back home. That would be the only logical thing to do. I must get . . . *home*!

Chapter 6

A NUMBNESS OVERTOOK ME as I drove from the parking lot. Four o'clock. I had hoped to miss the rush-hour traffic, the stand-still flow of cars, trucks, and buses that never yielded to any urgency of spirit. But missing that stressful element would have been too perfect, too ideal.

I was a small-town boy in a metropolis, out of place and out of time, only because of what was going on back home. Home: where nearly everybody knew my face and name; where, on return visits, I'd be greeted by a multitude of friends and acquaintances who, in their genial Southern manner, always wished me well but asked almost in concert:

"When are you coming back to Bayden to stay?" It was as though they were asking in my mother's behalf.

A horn honked somewhere. Oh, the light was green. I hadn't seen it. The hum of traffic was competing with my thinking.

The people back home — it seemed paradoxical that they wished me much success and contentment in my new location, yet would suggest that I should think of moving back to the town of my birth where I would "certainly be happier." Again, without conscious knowledge, they would be affirming my mother's desire. Yet, I appreciated their caring, and I welcomed their courtesies each time I returned.

A screech of tires. Someone was in too much of a hurry — impatient. The driver nearly hit the car on his left. And I was in the middle lane, crowded on either side, and unable to move. Trapped!

At the Bayden drugstore, Hedwick's Pharmacy — a local meeting place for many of the townspeople, where they sipped on coffee or soft drinks, ate sandwiches and pastries, and exchanged or embellished tidbits of information — I'd receive inquiries about my mother, my son, and any new romantic interest I'd encountered. At the local florist, I'd receive a hug and teasing from the owner. She'd ask when I was going to take her back to Texas with me. Maxine knew my family well. Many floral arrangements had been taken to Mama's from her shop.

My aunts had a major account with Maxine; they bought flowers for nearly everybody, so of a certainty my mother never lacked for fresh bouquets. Fresh bouquets — cut flowers; potted plants with profuse blooms, rock gardens with assorted greenery. Mama loved them all and called them "beautiful," stretching out and underscoring the first syllable as though each offering were more special than the last.

My apartment complex ahead. The palm trees beckoned, strangely situated beside live oaks, ash trees, maples,

and sycamores: as though out of place, unordered, as if incorrectly planted and positioned, though effectively arranged in keeping with the landscape and location, for this climate was sub-tropical. Why did I notice; why did I care? A few lifeless leaves held fast to the topmost branches of the sycamore: holding on, holding on.

Into the driveway, and I parked my tan car in its designated spot. Out of the driver's seat, I locked the doors with a turn of the key, and walked across the parking lot to the steps. A strange black dog snarled at me and tried to follow. I rebuked him, but he was insistent, so I sent him away with a kick — something I ordinarily would not have done. I usually fed strays, but this dog was frightening and appeared aggressive and mean. He looked back and growled. I had never seen him before. Why was he following me? He sat on his haunches, lifted his head, and howled.

Mama had said that her dog Lucy howled the night that Papa died, a half hour before Mama Sarah's driver came to tell her the news. Why was I remembering? Up three flights of stairs. My neighbor waved at me over her laundry basket. *No, please! Not the long, cold wave of death. . . .*

Inside the apartment: 4:45 p.m.

I dropped my briefcase in the brown chair and fell across the bed. I took several deep breaths to organize my thoughts. The phone on the walnut nightstand begged to be dialed. I punched in the familiar number. Maxine answered.

"Oh, hello, Sonny. Yes, I have a large potted chrysanthemum with a lot of yellow blossoms. Yes, we can deliver it today. It's almost quitting time. I'll decorate it especially for you and take it out there myself. So sorry your mother is worse. Your aunts told me."

I thanked her and hung up the phone. It didn't matter that Mama might never see the flowers. They'd told me that she kept her eyes closed most of the time now. Light hurt them. They were sore and dry, and so red. Still, somehow, Mama would know that the flowers were *"beau-*tiful." She'd think that, anyhow.

I could not understand my torture. If this was my personal hell, it seemed much more than I deserved. I would question that later — my offense, its penalty — and try to offer whatever recompense might be required. *These flowers — would they be the first ones for her funeral? Would this last chrysanthemum from me be the first of many to be borne to her resting place? Oh God, don't let her death knell come from me!*

Didn't I want her well and happy and healthy? Yet, didn't I also want her to be as she wanted to be, whatever and wherever that was — in that "mysterious realm" with Daddy, as his favorite poem, "Thanatopsis," suggested — "sustained and soothed by an unfaltering trust . . . lying down to peaceful . . ."?

Unconsciously, I must have been dialing Mama's number. My sister Francine's voice startled me to harsh reality. "I think she's asleep, Sonny. I've been here for about half an hour; just got off work. Robert has just now left. He's working tonight, but will be calling every half hour or so. He talked to Mama a few minutes ago — just before he left. He couldn't get her to say anything, but she nodded and shook her head to his questions. That's about all. She was conscious, I think, but very still. Her eyes were closed — still are — and her breathing is shallow." I heard Francine swallow. "Dee said Mama did manage a few words with you when you called earlier this afternoon."

"Yes." I was choking. ". . . asked me to come home, Frannie."

"Well, you know how that is, Baby Brother. She's wanted you to come home every day ever since you left five years ago. Don't let that bother you."

But it *did* bother me. It had always bothered me, and would be an emotional thorn as long as I had memory. But I'd have to work that out later, if a resolution were available to me. *I'd have to work that out later*. I couldn't dwell on selfish matters.

I could readily perceive Francine's sorrow, though she was crying quietly. She was offering me her strength when she really needed mine. Her husband had died two years ago after a lingering illness, and she must be reliving that pain, watching Mama.

Francine had tended to me when I was a baby. She had fed me, changed my clothes, scolded me, and even spanked me occasionally, but had always rewarded me with the whitest smile in my remembrance. Her whole face seemed to open up. She had been so beautiful, and always wore such colorful clothes when younger. I remembered her black, shiny hair and her fine features, her sparkling blue eyes — the gardenias she wore in her hair, and their distinctive perfume. Even now, she was smiling — I was certain — but through drowning eyes.

"Sonny, it's so bad — so very bad. Go ahead, if you want to. *Cry*."

She knew me all too well. The thirsty point of an imaginary knife ripped at my soul. But I couldn't cry. I ached all over, but the luxury of tears was out of reach; they would not come. Later, a million or more would fall, but now

I couldn't manage to move the cloud. I coughed. "Has Dr. Jackson been?"

"Yes. He took us aside — Robert, Dee, Joseph, Rebecca Ann, and me. Priscilla was feeling quite bad herself; Marvin took her home to put her to bed. Dr. Jackson told us that Mama might last a few more days. Couldn't give us a lot of hope, though. Without the tube — well, hardly anything left now." Then a shift in her tone: "Are you coming home?"

"As soon as I can make arrangements, Frannie. To be truthful, I've been so torn today between what to do and what not to do. You understand?" I knew she did. "I feel besieged by something I can't identify, Frannie. I can't explain it."

"I know, Sonny, but don't be hard on yourself. What is happening with Mama is nothing that you can change. Your being here wouldn't alter what has been done or what's happening now." Francine realized that I had become addicted to guilt. Perhaps she, more than all the others, knew and understood that aspect of my inner being; she had seen my soul bared.

Francine knew that, however well-intentioned, my bent of striving for and demanding perfection had probably precipitated the separation that had led to my divorce. Poor, pauper-clad excuses could not suffice any more than the most elaborate alibis. And though not solely responsible, neither was I blameless. Francine, perhaps more than any of the others — and maybe because she was so approachable — had consoled me during that time, though I had resisted sympathy.

Pride, love, embarrassment: the scandal of estrangement, the dissolution of something that we all had held sacred:

marriage, "till death do us part. . . ."

Mama could not understand; she never would accept the fact that Jill and I were not together. We *had* to work it out; we had to compromise; we must reconcile all differences and put everything aside that might mar the sanctity of sacred trust, commitment.

"That poor little boy —" she had lamented, referring to our son, "he needs a mother and father together." Thirteen years ago, it happened. Nathan was now twenty.

Nathan, the author's son, at seven (1972), during the time of his parents' separation.

Francine was still talking. "Did you hear me, Sonny? I said, 'Have you eaten anything today?'" She knew that any distress killed my appetite.

"Well, a little lunch — but my stomach is in such a fix I don't believe I can eat anything now. Maybe some soup after I try to rest a little. What time is it, Frannie — there?"

"Six-thirty. Wait, someone's at the door." A pause, and Frannie was back on the line. "Some lovely yellow chrysanthemums. Dee said Maxine brought them — have your name on them. Very nice, Sonny — decorated so beautifully: pretty blue-and-yellow bow, green-and-blue foil wrapping, and numerous swirls. When Mama wakes up, we'll show it all to her."

When Mama wakes up. Francine was exercising strenuous optimism for me. She was good that way; she would even smile her way through sorrow to help someone else through a difficult time.

I got off the line, insisting that she call me if any change was noted. She promised that she or someone else would. She said good-bye only after I had convinced her that I was going to be all right. She had wanted me to call a neighbor to be with me; she didn't want me to be alone.

But I had to be alone. I could not take on any more pressure. Social amenities would be required if a neighbor came to keep me company, and I didn't have the sense or energy right now to exercise proper etiquette.

Chapter 7

I STRETCHED OUT ON THE BED and closed my eyes
against the glare of light forcing its way from behind the
brown-and-white draperies. One undisciplined beam was
blinding me. I shrank from it — a light that usually, if not so
harsh, I would have welcomed. I liked light. I liked bright-
ness. But some of my brightest hours had been touched by
sadness.

A hundred bells rang at once. It was the phone. The
digital clock on the nightstand said 9:30 p.m. That would be
10:30 Mama's time. It was dark inside my apartment. Even
the blinding glare had forsaken me.

I'd had a fitful sleep since I'd talked to Francine. How
could I have slept with so much on my mind? I was supposed
to be getting ready for the trip home. Bells again.

I was wet with a putrid perspiration, the ingredients
of guilt or some disquieting notions. I didn't know which. I
switched on the lamp and snatched the phone from the table.

In my haste, I sent one of the framed photographs crashing to the floor. I would see to that later. I would see to so *many* things later.

I heard Joseph's voice. "Sonny, I think you'd better go ahead and make definite plans to come on home. Guess now we should have asked you to come on earlier in the week. Sorry about that. Mama's a whole lot worse. It's happening a lot faster than the doctors thought. Dee can't rouse her at all. Her breathing is short and quick. Her color is bad."

Then he stopped. I waited an eternity for him to continue. "Don't know, frankly, if she can hold out for you to get here, Sonny." Then he sighed, but increased his volume: "Don't know how much longer she can last."

"*. . . how much longer she can last!*" Joseph was telling me that our mother was dying. Why hadn't I made airline reservations earlier in the week? Why wasn't I there by her side now, with the others — where I belonged?

"I'll catch a plane as soon as I can, Joseph. I'll call you as soon as I know, so you or someone else can meet me in Kennington. I'll let you know immediately — and you call me right back if there's any change — and, please, don't keep anything from me. Ah — is the doctor coming? Oh — has anyone called Priscilla — and is Robert there — and Rebecca Ann?" As if from this distance I could direct the moves! But my brothers and sisters had too often deferred to me, to my wishes, to my whims. I was remembering and regretting, lamenting.

Joseph again; the volume of his voice, though normal, sounded threatening and loud: "Robert's left work to come home. We just called him. And the doctor is with Mama now.

We've called Priscilla, too. She's trying to get here. And Rebecca Ann is on her way back. She had to get away for a while — couldn't stand to watch Mama so still." Then his voice grew soft.

"Brother, it's bad for all of us. Know it must be worse for you, with you out there so far away and alone." Joseph was abandoning his usual stronger-than-strong image and was revealing a trait he often kept inside; he was venting his feelings, though in a subdued manner: "Wish you'd call a friend or someone to be with you while you get ready to come home. Hate for you to be all by yourself." With that, he said good-bye.

Joseph, just four years older than I, had saved me from drowning when I was a child, but he could not save me now. The cruel waters were again dark and deep; this time, I was way out of reach.

* * * * * *

Trying every major airline, I discovered almost in horror that no flight from San Antonio to Kennington could be booked until the following day. A flight did leave San Antonio for Raleigh-Durham (a hundred miles from Bayden), the reservations clerk told me, but it had left earlier this evening, at 6 p.m.

Now, I wouldn't be able to get to Mama before tomorrow night. "Why, God?" A partisan something within me hated and loved at the same time, destroying whatever inner unity I had attempted to gather. But I was helpless.

"Sorry, Mr. Ellis, no flight until 1:05 tomorrow afternoon. All flights to Kennington, North Carolina, connect to and from Atlanta tonight. You'd have to spend tonight and most of tomorrow in the terminal and then connect to Kennington at 6 p.m. Eastern time. If you could have left at three this afternoon, I could have given you a more direct flight through Dallas-Fort Worth, arriving Kennington at 11:50 tonight. Sorry. Shall I go ahead and book you on tomorrow's one-o-five flight?"

A dozen sighs before I could answer.

"Did you understand me, Mr. Ellis?"

I answered the pleasant young woman, telling her that I did understand, and, yes, I did want to be booked on tomorrow's flight. I gave her all the information required, and she repeated flight numbers, times, and layovers, which I promptly wrote down. Then I called home. Robert answered the phone.

"Hello, Buddyroe," (an affectionate name for me).

"How'd you know it would be me, Robert?"

"Just did — I know how you are."

I immediately told him of my flight plans and the difficulty I'd had. Any change, Robert — in Mama?" I wanted to know, but some iron-like shield inside my brain barred the reception of any news worse than what I'd already learned. I felt the pangs of passive acceptance. I knew that any change had to be bad. Dr. Mallison hadn't held much back.

But Robert, in his mild and cautionary manner, had tried to protect my feelings on numerous occasions. He had always tempered the bad news with a reason for hope. Only eighteen months older than Joseph, and therefore about six years my senior, Robert had always been my defender, my champion. A peacemaker of sorts, he was easygoing and outwardly very gregarious, yet inwardly serious and afflicted by the same pain we all felt.

"Any change?" He acknowledged my question. "Well, Mama really *is* a lot worse, Sonny. But there's nothing you can do — nothing that anyone can do. She is not in any pain right now. We can be thankful for that, because she has been especially miserable for the past three days — or more like the whole week."

The "whole week" which Robert cited seemed more like a year to me; this year, like an eternity.

"Her eyes are closed, Sonny, but she did respond to my questions this afternoon before I went to work. Shook her head and seemed to respond correctly to what I asked. Knew my voice. When I asked if this was 'Joseph talking,' she shook her head no. When I said 'Robert,' she nodded yes. She couldn't talk, but was aware of what was going on. I asked her again about the hospital — and I repeated that twice to make certain she understood me. She shook her head in a very definite no. Now, I'm afraid she's out. Can't get her to move even her head. Dee says that her feet are cold, sort of blue in color, and —"

I stopped him. "*Blue*? Oh, no, that means . . ."

He wouldn't let me finish. "Now don't get upset. You know we've all hoped for so long that she'd soon be out of her misery; and we've tried everything she'd let us try to get her better."

"I know, Robert, but it's so hard — what did the doctor say tonight?"

"Well, he said that it couldn't be more than a few more hours. Dee keeps feeling of her face and is wiping it with a cool cloth, and is putting ointment on her lips. They're parched from dryness, I guess. Sounded like she mumbled your name a minute or so ago — oh, sorry, Sonny, shouldn't have told you *that* —"

Bothered by his own utter honesty, Robert stopped short. His voice cracked, but he hastened before I could respond: " Uh, . . . Frannie's been holding her hand. She does seem to know that we're here. She has a little grip left, but it's clear that she's sinking."

Then, in an obvious effort to support me as so many times before, Robert's voice became almost stern. "Now look, Sonny, go ahead and try to get some rest. I'll call you if you want me to, in about an hour — or you call here — anything that will make you feel better. But I wish you'd try to *sleep*. If you can't leave until after lunchtime tomorrow, you ought to relax some. Now, stop pacing the floor. I know how you are. Try to relax — at least *try*. Some of us will meet you at the airport —at what time did you say?"

I repeated my schedule, between sighs and hesitations in my speech pattern which I could not control. Robert was patient and gave me plenty of time to recap pertinent facts and some that were not so important. He indicated that talking was good for me, since it appeared that I was not going to relax.

"Go ahead, Sonny. Tell me again, so I'll be sure to have it all. I'm writing it down so there'll be no mistakes."

"All right, Robert. Can't get there before 10:35 tomorrow night, your time. I'll be on Piedmont Flight 281. Have a layover in Dallas for three and a half hours — change planes there and leave at 5:20 — arrive in Charlotte at 9:28, and have a fifteen-minute stop there. Best I could do." My voice broke.

"I understand, Sonny — go ahead."

"No direct flight was available, except to Raleigh-Durham; and honestly, I can't stand that two-hour drive from there to Bayden. Even if I flew directly to Raleigh, I'd make no better time, because arriving at 8 p.m. there, plus the two-hour drive home, would have me arriving little more than a half hour earlier. Thirty minutes from Kennington Airport to Bayden will be better on all of us, I think. Now don't forget, I'll be arriving at 10:35 p.m. — in Kennington — on Piedmont 281."

It occurred to me that all these details weren't necessary, but I felt better being able to make logical order out of time and direction. I knew that Robert understood.

Chapter 8

TEN O'CLOCK AND I STILL HADN'T PACKED! What would I take? A dark suit for the funeral, a brown-and-beige for greeting relatives, a burgundy-and-blue for the formal viewing; ties to match, belts, shirts, and shoes — and socks. I must not forget coordinating socks.

Another outfit or two for the visits I'd be expected to make, even during these circumstances; but what would I wear on the plane? Oh, the double-breasted navy blazer with the plaid trousers.

I should not care how I looked, but I did. I couldn't alter the core of my personality, even in an emergency; and my family would expect me to be myself. But matching everything, coordinating and planning everything — how could I be so methodical? My mother was critically ill, probably dying, and I was being methodical. *Perhaps being methodical would delay that which was bound to come. If only . . .*

But Mama had cared for fashions, too. If I were fastidious, the trait must have come from her. I could well remember musing over photographs taken of her when she was young, in which she wore large bows and ribbons of fashion in her hair, or wide-brimmed hats perched on her head, trimmed in satin and lace and netting; with matching, long flowing dresses; and gloves.

I remembered how it was said of her: "Eva never wore the same outfit twice. And she always looked so lovely — everything looked good on her with that tiny, tiny waist — and that white, white skin."

And I could remember, too — even when she had someone else to do it for her — how she used to iron my shirts to a comfortable crispness, insisting that they must be as wrinkle-free as possible — and that they needed "a mother's touch." And, then, when one unwanted crease dared present itself, she would laugh softly and advise: "Well, it won't be seen on a galloping horse."

Mama used to spend hours in that ironing room . . . but she had chided me many times because it "took forever" for me to get dressed for a special occasion. I was "taking forever" now. . . .

Two suitcases and one garment bag should be more than enough, but I had to be sure that I didn't run out of clothes. I set about folding and packing, sorting and resorting, organizing and reorganizing. More light; I needed more light. This one on, that one on, until every lamp and overhead light in the apartment chased away even the suggestion of a shadow.

Eight shirts — maybe ten — one for each outfit and some extra. These didn't have the finish that Mama used to give them . . . why did it matter? She hadn't done my shirts in years, but . . .

I sat momentarily in a side chair by the bed, took a few breaths, and began once more the frantic pace. Packing should be done slowly. I couldn't leave until tomorrow afternoon, so why the rush? *Death couldn't wait for me.*

Why didn't someone call? They promised to keep me informed. *Ten-forty-five.* Had it taken me that long to sort my things? Halfway packed. I must hurry. Where was my burgundy tie? I had to have that. Why wasn't it on the rack with all the others? I'd looked through dozens without finding it. Oh, there — on the floor behind one of the suitcases.

Maybe some music would help. I switched on the stereo to my favorite music station. "For Easy Listening," they called it — *but nothing was easy about this situation.* The strains of some mellow chamber music caught my ear. A violin superimposed a haunting refrain. *Mama used to play the violin.*

Older family members had told me about the music parties they had enjoyed at Mama's ancestral home when, at my grandmother Sarah's bidding, Mama would entertain those present with her superb musicianship at the piano, at the parlor organ, and with her operatic soprano voice. They had told me about the proficiency with which Mama had played the Cremona violin — a violin given to her by her father — handed down in the family — which had been stolen by a most unlikely person not long after her marriage, and sold for a "mere pittance," but by necessity, it had been told.

The lead violinist on this recording was playing so well, superimposing the melody line of Beethoven's "Ode to Joy." Sadly, I had never heard Mama draw music from the violin, but I *had* heard her play the piano and sing. She had often reminded us: "To sing a song will right a wrong." When very young, I did not comprehend the exact meaning of the words; but the rhyme itself was music; and because Mama had made the statement, I knew it must be true. *If only the proverb could be applied to all circumstances. She would contend that it could, but I did not know how. I did not feel like singing.*

As I rose from adjusting the volume on the stereo, I met the reflection of my face in the glass covering the large picture of my mother's house. She had given this to me on my last visit. It had been one of my gifts to her several Christmases past, and she had wanted me to have it to remind me of home.

I hadn't needed any reminders, but I had accepted the picture gratefully. My father had designed and added three second-story dormer windows to both sides of the house during a remodeling program. Three of these showed plainly in the green roof, and jutted proudly above the whiteness of the house. I had often played behind those dormers as a child, darting back and forth from one to the other, much as my face now shifted position in the glass with my movements.

My face against the picture of the house, distorted by the glass and reflected back, seemed thinner and paler to me than I had thought. Perspiration again soaked my clothes. I must take a shower.

The warm water was soothing, but less than relaxing. A quick shower this time; I'd take a more thorough one later. A quick towel-dry, and I pulled on some comfortable white shorts and a red T-shirt, rubbing my bare feet against the short nap of the brown carpet.

Eleven-fifteen. I must finish packing. Shirts and jackets in the garment bag, remaining coats and trousers in suitcases, along with shoes and socks — and, there, I was finished — or almost. Any forgotten items would be added tomorrow morning after I'd had time to reassess my selections. I moved the suitcases to the living room and laid the garment bag, with zipper open, across one of the gold-and-white couches in front of the large window. Gathering the outfit I'd wear on the plane, I placed it, along with socks and shoes, on the matching gold-and-white loveseat.

Everything lay in readiness — except *me*.

Chapter 9

I MUST CHECK ON MAMA. The phone was subtly mocking. Its news could only be bad, but it possessed the power to excite or quiet me, to alarm or reassure. It even had the power to refuse.

A busy signal! Someone else must be checking on Mama, or someone at Mama's was relaying the bad news of her condition — or maybe calling the doctor. I wished they'd hurry. I replaced the phone to its position on the night table. I'd try again in five minutes.

Wait, something was missing among the photographs on the table. Mama's picture! I'd heard something fall earlier — it couldn't be. But yes, there behind the table, lodged between it and the wall was the familiar gold frame. I retrieved the picture with now shaking fingers. The broken glass cut my hand. A single sliver had broken away from Mama's face, her face of three years ago when she had been relatively well and happy and we'd all been together during

her eighty-seventh birthday celebration — one of six identical pictures made, one for every child. I had broken Mama's picture. *Could this be a sign?*

Outside, a dog howled. Must be the strange, black dog I had seen earlier. I wished he would go back to wherever it was he belonged — away from me.

I lifted the phone again. No busy signal this time. A knock on the door. Who could that be? My watch said eleven-thirty. I replaced the phone and walked to the door. It was my neighbor Greg.

"Saw all your lights on, Sonny, and wondered if something was wrong. Lisa said that you seemed in such a rush when you came home this afternoon. Don't mean to pry, but it's unusual for you to have all the lights on." Then, noting that I was obviously getting ready for a trip, he added, "Something I can help you with?"

I thanked him and related the events of the day and evening. I had eaten meals with Greg and his wife on occasion, and we had attended a few concerts together; but our lives were spent in separate occupational pursuits. We were friends, but not really close. I had chosen a solitary life out of preference rather than necessity. In conversation, I had mentioned my mother's illness, but not its severity. So Greg and Lisa knew a little of the torment I suffered being so far away from the family, but I had never let them know the intensity.

Now Greg seemed to be the sounding board I needed, though one I had not anticipated and did not want. Both Francine and Joseph had insisted that I have a neighbor or someone sit with me while I waited. Maybe Greg could help. Motioning for him to have a seat on the upholstered deacon's bench, I sat across from him in the white rocker, in easy reach of the silent phone.

"Sonny, are you sure there isn't something I can do?" Greg was invading my selfish privacy. "Maybe if you talked about it, you'd feel better." I didn't know the strain showed. I must really look wrung out. Greg was being kind; I knew that.

"I don't know if talking about the gruesome details will help, Greg."

"I didn't mean *that*."

"Oh, I know. I was just reflecting. My mother has always been so strong. She always looked after everybody else, and now she's helpless and —" I had to stop to swallow. "She might not be here much longer. I expect the next phone call to be the one telling me that she's — you know."

Greg nodded. "I understand."

I took a few deep breaths and sat motionless in the rocker, holding my head in my hands. I had rocked away many a crisis, but not this one. 'Just let me die. *Just let me die!*"

Greg was puzzled. "What are you saying, Sonny?"

"'*Just let me die.*' My mother has said that so often this past year. I suppose those words will haunt me for the rest of my life." I choked. I was still watching the phone, wanting it to ring, but hoping at the same time that it would not. Greg's earlier intrusion had stopped me from dialing. Now I waited for the sound that would startle me and hated the silence that kept me in suspense. As long as the phone didn't ring, Mama was holding on. But should I wish her to

hold on to something which she no longer controlled? Should I want her to hold on for us, when she wanted to be free?

I stared at my watch again. *Twelve midnight. One o'clock Mama's time.* I double-checked the time. The digital clock beside the phone said 12:02. I couldn't wait any longer. I must call.

Greg nodded his support as I reached for the phone. I wanted him to leave, but how could I tell him? If the news I got was really bad, I didn't want him there to share it — it was too personal. And if the news was good — but how could it be good? I didn't want to relate anything to anybody. Greg seemed to read my feelings. He got up from the bench, raised his hand in a quiet good-bye, and mouthed an inaudible but unmistakable amenity: "If you need anything, call."

I thanked him and turned to dial my mother's number. I heard the door close as I made connection. Robert came on the line. My own voice was oddly calm. "Robert, tell me, how is Mama? I hate so much for her to be suffering."

Robert was silent for a moment. Then he told me what I dreaded, yet what something inside me hoped to hear. "Well, Sonny, you don't have to worry about her suffering any more."

"You mean — ?"

"Yes, 12:50 our time — about fifteen minutes ago. I was going to wait until morning to let you know, hoping you might rest some tonight — but since you've called —"

"Are you sure she's really gone, Robert? How can you know?" Maybe I was overperceiving; maybe I was implementing that abiding hope I'd been taught to use; perhaps my question would somehow allow us to keep her a while longer. But a too-familiar chill crawled across my soul. "How can you *know*, Robert?" I repeated.

"Just take my word. You *can* know. She passed away very quietly, Sonny. No struggle at all. You can be thankful for that. She just took one deep breath, a long sigh, and that was it."

"Was anybody holding on to her when it happened, Robert? I hate to think of Mama dying without a comforting hand." Her own hand had soothed our hurts and had touched our brows in love and, when needed, had corrected us with gentle discipline. The touch of her hand had made everything right. Even fevers fled from her touch, and the cold of winter had shied away when she tucked the covers about our necks. Yes, her touch had made everything right. I wanted her to feel that same response from us. My hand wasn't long enough to reach, but my heart . . .

Robert's answer interrupted my self-pity or whatever else it was I felt. "Yes, Sonny. Four of her children were with her when it happened. I was holding her hand; Joseph was stroking her face. Francine and Rebecca Ann were at the foot of the bed rubbing her legs and feet. Dee was standing at the head of the bed, talking quietly to her. Priscilla was too sick to be here, but we've called her.

"They're just now taking Mama away." I heard the familiar catch in his voice, and he continued. "As I told you, we didn't want to tell you till morning, knowing how you are, and you being so far away." Robert was always the protecting brother, and never more so than now.

Something sounded and resounded in my head, an accusatory something I couldn't identify, unless it was guilt in other clothes: "Four of her children were with her when it happened." Priscilla would have been at Mama's bedside, too, but she had gone home sick this afternoon. And I, I was fifteen hundred miles away — *by choice*! And my mother had asked for me up until the last, and she had declared her love for *me* with the little strength she had left.

I had always thought of myself as the dutiful son, but I had failed my mother. I had turned deaf ears to her plea: "Why don't you come on home?" The question came from a dozen directions and whirled together in a buzzing in my ears. Then Robert's voice broke through: "Sonny, I do wish you'd call someone to stay with you."

"I'll be all right, Robert." I had never been a good liar.

Chapter 10

$\mathcal{S}$ATURDAY AFTERNOON, DECEMBER 7, 1985. The plane ride from San Antonio to Dallas - Fort Worth was uneventful, though I felt detached from all surroundings, or centered somewhere in a vacuum. Never had "going home" been so grim an experience.

I had left San Antonio International at 1:15, almost on schedule, and though I knew about the layover in Dallas, the three-and-a-half hours there seemed interminable. At 5:45, I was in the air again, flying toward Charlotte, expected arrival time: 9:28 p.m. Eastern time.

Now, a little more than an hour to go, and I'd touch down in Kennington.

The airspace between Charlotte and Kennington was unusually rough and rainy. The plane seemed tossed about, as on a stormy sea, producing an appropriate mood for this trip home. Somehow, I had gotten through the night — but

I didn't know how. Greg and Lisa had cooked breakfast for me, which I'd had to decline. I had taken a cab to the airport, and had done all the necessary things for departure.

Robert had called early, at seven this morning, regarding funeral arrangements — asking my approval of eulogizers, musicians, what Mama was to be dressed in, her casket type, and all manner of details that seemed cold and deliberate but were essential to the proper carrying out of interment.

Everybody in the family wanted me to be satisfied concerning the most critical details, even to the kind of flowers and the size of the casket spray. Once, years ago, before such arrangements had become necessary, I had been selfish enough to want to attend to all these matters personally. I had thought of doing this almost to the exclusion of the others — in the name of love, naturally, somehow thinking I had that right, being "Mama's baby." Rebecca Ann had justifiably chastened me: "Sonny, I think that's asking a little too much. Mama has five other children, you know."

I just wanted Mama to have the best, and I'd wanted to make preparations well in advance, before emotions got in the way; but I must also have had a rather exalted opinion of my own tastes. Now, thinking back, I could blame immaturity for my ill-advised assertion. Ironically, I would have no say now, except to make suggestions and then agree with the selections made by my brothers and sisters.

But they would see to it, as many in the South describe such preparations, "that Mama was put away properly." I knew that. Yet, Rebecca Ann, perhaps remembering our conversation of years ago, and being ever conscious of what many called my "discriminating preferences," and

wanting me to be satisfied, had asked the others: "What if Sonny gets here and doesn't like what we've done?"

"We'll just change everything," Robert had remarked.

Certainly, they were all being too considerate, but I was glad that they cared and wanted to please me. I had told Robert: "Just be sure that Mama is put away nicely. Pick out the very best for her — she always did for us." I didn't need to insist; they wanted as much for Mama as I did — probably more. They had been with her; I had not.

Mama had died early this morning, or just before midnight, depending on time zones. It seemed bizarre that she had died late Friday night *my* time but early Saturday morning *her* time. A light-year seemed lodged between Eastern and Central times. The papers would say December 7, but I'd always think of her death as occurring ten minutes before midnight, Friday, December 6. It would be branded in my heart and mind.

The plane was landing. It was 10:45 p.m. I'd had to move my watch up one hour. Piedmont 281 would be setting down at Gate 4, the airline representative told me. My family would be waiting for me there. I felt cold, even before the plane touched down.

But the coldness was more than physical. The pilot had informed the passengers of a 40° temperature reading on the ground and had said that the weather had cleared. No rain. The runway lights weren't veiled with the fog I had expected, but appeared dim nonetheless.

Feeling listless and tired, I began deplaning with automatic motions, forcing an occasional smile to fellow passengers crowding the aisle for exit. I blew out several

Nathan at 20 (1985), as he looked during that difficult time.

breaths as I waited for those ahead of me to move forward. Finally I was at the door. A quick good-bye and thank-you to the attendants, and I was rushing through the chute to the terminal.

Scanning the lobby of Gate 4, I focused on the familiar faces of my brother Robert; his oldest son, William; and his wife, Janene; Robert's youngest son, Bob, who had visited his grandmother every day; and my own son, Nathan.

Nathan's eyes were the first to meet mine. Taller by only an inch, his six-foot-one frame seemed to tower over me as we embraced. He stood back to look at me through swollen eyes, still holding me by the shoulders. A lone tear dropped to his lip.

"I'm so sorry, Daddy. I loved Grandmother Eva so much." I nodded and swallowed the lump that was forming in my throat.

Robert extended his hand and then an arm around my neck, and asked if I were "all right." He knew that I wasn't, but offered emotional strength with his question. A special embrace from twenty-year-old Bob, who, being the same age as Nathan, seemed to feel special affection for me and gave real meaning to the title "Uncle." A hug from

William and Janene, and silent exchanges of caring from everybody; and Nathan and Bob were off to get my luggage.

Chapter 11

T HE THIRTY-MINUTE RIDE TO BAYDEN seemed endless. My nephews and niece talked quietly in the backseat. Robert drove slowly and told me about the arrangements, how good Mama looked, how she was dressed, and other details. His words came as from a great distance. Nathan, sitting between Robert and me, occasionally squeezed my arm, communicating a son's love, understanding and empathizing. My voice came involuntarily: "Can we go by to see her, Robert?"

"They've closed the funeral home for the night, Sonny. And I believe it'll be better on you if you wait till morning. I'll take you down early. All right?"

A reluctant yes from me, then Robert enumerated the family members who were waiting for me at Mama's. We'd see them, then he'd take me to his house where they'd prepared a guest room for me. "Didn't think you'd want to stay at Mama's — but if you'd rather —" The closeness of her death was too much. Robert instinctively knew that and was looking out for me.

The sign read "Pleasant Lane," and just ahead of us down the dirt road the big house stood among the giant oaks and magnolias — framed and reframed by their protecting, sheltering stance: a picture for my swollen eyes; a memory for my tormented soul: a contented, fair haven that had offered peace, security.

In my youth and young adulthood, I had found every splendor in that old house. Built in the mid- to late-1800s, it was originally the home of a Confederate hero with a connection to my family, and therefore of historical significance. To me, it was simply "my mama's home": a humble, ancient dwelling, but one of unsurpassed, sentimental importance. It was now bathed by a December moon whose glow belied the somber mood that prevailed.

I could almost see Mama opening the door, walking toward me, calling me by name. Robert was asking: ". . . you all right, Sonny?" I had not heard him speak. He did not need an answer; he knew what I was feeling.

Into the cedar-lined drive, past a dozen or more cars in the yard — plus almost as many trucks and station wagons — and we stopped at the brick walk. Looming toward me from the long, lighted porch was the ominous green-and-white wreath of death. Reticulated, close-set banister supports surrounded the perimeter of the porch, along with decorative, hand-carved moldings above and balustrades below. These Victorian effects and the several fluted posts cast strange, pierced and segmented shadows upon the steps and the ground. This sight forbade my entrance, whereas usually it invited me.

I braced myself against the dashboard as Robert pulled the emergency brake. He always set the brake when he stopped his car; but this time it seemed more definite, more determined: absolute. "Ready to get out, Daddy?" Nathan observed my nervous hands.

"Give me a minute." I inhaled and tapped the dashboard with a cadence from my subconscious. The green chairs, especially Mama's favorite rocker, were vacant, as were the swing and wicker settees and various other benches and chairs. All of these remained in fixed, patterned units, and symmetry — with their matching tables — according to Mama's preferred balance, her artistic eye. Dee and Rebecca Ann had been careful not to move anything out of place, knowing that I would notice and be disturbed.

The green-colored flower boxes and hanging baskets were devoid of blooms, but it was December — I shouldn't wonder.

I heard myself asking about Brandy; he was not on the porch. Robert explained that last night, right after Mama "passed away," Brandy had cried and howled, had crawled away on all fours, and had then run to hide in one of the barns, and could not be persuaded to come back to the house — nor to eat. Bob hastened to tell me that no one knew what had happened to Tammy, but that some of the grandchildren were on the lookout for her. She would show up eventually, they were certain. *Somehow the dog and cat knew that their mistress was gone and would not be returning.*

A sound of closing car doors, and I was being guided up the walk. A dry leaf trembled on the bottom step. I stopped to look, almost wanting to pick it up. The others paused and waited until I was ready. My equilibrium was tortured

by something within and without. My nerves turned on full swell, and my whole foundation seemed shaken. Robert gripped my arm to steady me. Nathan's hand was on my shoulder.

Someone opened the storm door; and I, in a daze, walked down the wide, endless hall, upon its blue-and-red wool runner; and under three precisely spaced, dimly lit ceiling lamps. I was led past the antique hall rack and other familiar pieces of furniture: heirloom marble-top tables holding groupings of Dresden figurines, glass and porcelain vases, miniature pictures in their gold frames; fern stands; and upholstered chairs of silk and cut velvet, which now, for all their former warmth, seemed to welcome me with hollow consolation.

And there, heavy on the papered walls (some having their own frame lights) were many of the familiar, ancestral photographs and paintings of heraldic symbols, emblems, and coats of arms emblazoned with rich colors. They claimed their stations, demonstrating notable lineage — and, at this moment, appeared almost fearful, startling. Why must I observe such exhibits now? A thousand times before, I had passed them without looking, though I always knew they were there — watching.

In these impressive displays, I remembered, our unpretentious mother did not place the same importance as did many others in her family. But these details were nevertheless part of the scene, and for years had been permanent fixtures in her surroundings — and ours: familiar, somehow friendly, even if lofty; but now reminding me too much of that which I did not want to see, to know, to realize. Something — *someone* — a valued presence — was missing from all this. But, of course.

I was being guided past and away from the imposing, weighty "ornaments" and their stately placements. I
felt cold. A turn to the left, and the door was opening.

With the warmth of her smile, but red of eye, my sister Francine greeted me from Mama's flower-filled sitting
room and reached out to embrace me. Inside, and she pointed out in particular a unique arrangement from a favorite
teacher who had kept in touch and had followed my career
with special interest — yellow roses, blue asters, and white
fuji mums in a blue-and-yellow vase, with dark green ferns
and a blue-and-white ribbon. My eyes registered every detail, but why? *As if doing so would relieve the pain.* The
card was signed simply: "Just because. Love, Louise Mid-
dleton."

Several table lamps lit the room in soft light. The
large, overhead fixture glowed with reflected light only and
spattered prism hues in every direction: so much color for
this mood.

Someone directed me toward an empty rocking chair
they'd reserved for me near the fireplace. The gas logs, set
on low, warmed and brightened that part of the room. I
instinctively moved my chair farther away from the heat
and removed my jacket, raising my hand to stay the gestures of help that cousins and nephews offered.

Mama's life-sized portrait, inside its ornate golden
frame, rested in half-light above the mantel and reached
toward the high ceiling. I could not bear to look at it, though
I myself had supervised its being hung there fifteen years
earlier — just after it had been painted. Mama had been sev-
enty-five, and elegant; she had on a velvet dress of deep,
blue violet with a self-fabric flower in hues of purple and violet

on her left shoulder; she wore a single strand of pearls around her neck with a diamond drop and small, matching earrings. Her auburn, silver-streaked hair lay in soft, lustrous waves; and was tied in a large bun at the back. The expression on her face was serious, but gentle and kind: fair and serene.

I was again remembering every detail, though I was disinclined to look — hoping not to be reminded further of the emptiness I felt.

Hugs and muddled phrases from family members and several close friends, offers of food, drink, and other amenities were extended — all catered to my comfort. Hope insisted that I have tea — or a soft drink — and some of her chicken salad, some pineapple cake, or some of my other favorite foods, which she had prepared. She understood when I said no, but continued to encourage me to eat something.

Nathan sat on the red velvet piano stool near me, where Mama had often sat. The glow from a crystal lamp shone on his face and hair. The large, antique "looking glass" — as Mama had called it — behind the old Baldwin piano caught Nathan's reflection, and sent it back as a younger version of me. Nathan touched my shoulder from time to time; and, as was typical of him, when sitting here, he depressed a piano key every now and then, bringing a bell-like tone from the sounding board, invoking a shudder from me.

Someone stilled his hand, and he looked at me as if to apologize. He joined in the conversation with cousins and with Joseph and Rebecca Ann. He would go home for the night — fifty miles away, where he resided with his mother — but would come back early in the morning to be with me.

Rebecca Ann's voice sounded hoarse. She had been trying not to cry. I rocked quietly and said little. I felt myself wanting to ask: "How's Mama?" I choked back the emotion that came with the thought. Robert observed my uneasiness and insisted that I go with him to his house; I needed to go to bed, he said.

"What time is it?" I heard myself asking.

"Twelve-thirty." Joseph nodded toward Mama's hand-carved English clock.

Chapter 12

A GRAY DAWN CREPT THROUGH THE DRAPES and edged its way toward the bed. I could visualize how earlier the advancing fog had caressed — then swallowed — everything it had touched. Harsh reality. I had not slept; I had heard sounds through the house all night. Apparently, none of Robert's family had slept soundly, either. Though I had heard soft voices throughout the night, there was still an aloneness I could not fathom. I felt enveloped by the same feeling now as my eyes focused on the maple dresser.

The clock said 6:15. I'd shower and shave and try not to disturb those who might be attempting to get a little sleep. But the house sounded too alive for anyone to be sleeping. *Too alive*. Why had my mind chosen those words? Such irony.

From the kitchen came the aroma of bacon and eggs and coffee. Sue was preparing breakfast. I didn't want to eat,

but I knew I needed to. It had been many hours since I'd had any food. I had not eaten the soup that I had promised Francine I'd try when she had spoken to me over the phone — only the night before last — but it seemed like days ago.

Bob had heard me moving about. He called, "Uncle Sonny, we're having breakfast now. We'll make yours whenever you're ready for it — but take your time." I thanked him and continued my grooming. I was tying my maroon-and-blue tie when Nathan opened the bedroom door.

"Good morning, Daddy. I've just gotten here. Ready for breakfast?" I nodded at his reflection in the mirror. He put both hands on my shoulders and turned me around to face him, then embraced me without speaking.

We walked together through the pine-paneled den, into the blue-and-white breakfast nook, and took our places at the kitchen table. A brass-and-crystal, tulip-shaped lamp, suspended by a swagging, adjustable brass chain, hung over the oak table. Sue had set special places for Nathan and me, and with her usual cordiality had squeezed fresh oranges for me. Robert was pouring my coffee and asking about cream as he held up the small blue-and-white container. Nathan told him yes for both of us; and said that he'd have sausage instead of bacon.

I took small bites of everything, while Robert and Bob engaged in conversation to encourage me to eat more. All the while, Nathan was patting my shoulder, making a joke here and there in an effort to ease my mind, still unable to hide the grief that had stolen his usual expression.

I knew that he felt sad at his grandmother's passing, but he also felt sad for me. He had been aware of my

turmoil and guilt. With the thumb and forefinger of his right hand, he squeezed the back of my neck in understanding, then pushed away from the table to help Sue clear away the dishes.

"Do you feel like going now?" Robert's voice was calm. "It's eight o'clock." I swallowed and nodded. Bob and Nathan would go with us. I went to the bedroom to get my gray jacket — and through habit, checked my teeth, popped a mint into my mouth — then joined the others in the den. Nathan had put on his tan blazer and was straightening his brown tie. Through the open door, down the brick steps, into the car, and we were headed toward Bayden Funeral Home. Mama would be there.

The two-mile trip to the funeral home required no more than ten minutes, but was nonetheless a ponderable time, as my heart seemed to beat in my throat and interfered with my breathing. This time, I sat between Robert and Nathan. In their own way, they each were expressing concern through occasional glances toward me and with a touch on my arm.

My nephew Bob sat in the back seat, and leaned forward with one hand on my shoulder, pointing out new housing projects and apartment complexes and commenting on how the area was progressing. He seemed intent on diverting my attention momentarily from the immediate trouble he knew I would soon be experiencing. His pleasant manner lifted me, and I was able to turn my head and smile in response; but I said nothing.

Through the residential district, down Second Street with its numerous oak trees, through town, and we were pulling into the driveway. There was the familiar structure

— the building of red bricks and white columns, large multi-paned windows and double doors — the funeral home where my mother was now resting. My watch said 8:25.

The sky had cleared, and the winter sun was warm — almost too warm — but an involuntary shiver overtook me. I was glad that there was no rain. Some of my older relatives had been heard to remark that rain nearly always came the day of an elderly person's funeral. Mama's memorial service would be held tomorrow afternoon. I wondered what that day would bring. I hoped it wouldn't rain, but she'd say I shouldn't concern myself with such matters.

"After all, the Lord's work shall be done." *Her voice; her words, in my head.*

Out of the car, and we were greeted by a friend I'd known for many years, who had married into our family but had recently dissolved the union. She had felt especially close to my mother; and, upon seeing me get out of Robert's car, she had pulled into the parking lot to speak to me. She looked sad, regretful. She seemed intent on seeing me, momentarily ignoring the others.

She walked up to me, embraced me quietly, then whispered, "Are you going to be all right?" I nodded and she stepped back to look at me, as though doubting my word.

"Really, I'll be all right," I assured her. Had I faltered more, she would have gone in with me to offer added support, even if uninvited; but she appeared satisfied that I was in good hands.

She squeezed my arm, spoke to the others, and was off to Sunday school, offering an apology for having interrupted.

Robert ushered me to the porch and to the double doors. The funeral director, James Merritt, opened the door, shook my hand, and with a reserved smile greeted me quietly but warmly in his long, Southern drawl: "Hey, Sonny."

With his arm around my neck, he pulled me closer, then took me again by the hand, stepped back, and opened the other door so we all could enter. He led us to an area adjacent to the large viewing room. I heard ethereal strings and the sound of a lonesome organ: piped-in music which seemed cold, calculated, impersonal, but convenient.

Victorian-style chairs and sofas of mahogany and velvet, and marble-top tables decorated the room — and all the adjoining ones; heavy curtains with gold-colored tassels framed the windows. Large-branched chandeliers hung from the ceiling, emitting dim light that played and pranced too gaily against hundreds of tear-drop crystals.

Rainbow colors; Mama had loved the sight of rainbows: "the promise after rain," she had often explained to the delighted grandchildren. Why was my mind choosing words like "delighted"? Nothing seemed delightful about where I was, why I was here.

A thick, multicolored carpet covered the major portion of the floor; but groupings of furniture were arranged around Persian rugs with small areas of hardwood flooring showing here and there. I had been here more than a hundred times before; I knew this place by heart. This time, my heart did not *want* to know it.

The interior air was dense with a fragrance almost too funereal, but appropriate. Several floral arrangements already stood in place, and Mr. Merritt remarked that one

of the florists had called to say that they were delivering more. I heard him speaking to Robert. Robert asked that they not disturb me, that they hold the flowers until later.

Chapter 13

AGAINST THE CREAM-COLORED WALL stood the blue-gray casket with its dense blanket of red roses and white carnations. The coverlet of flowers lay atop a full spread of delicate, green ferns supported by heavy, more substantial, foliage. An identical blanket of flowers and ferns stood to one side but some distance away. Together, when the time came, the two half-length coverlets would be draped over the full span of the casket top to soften the effect of the cold, blue-gray metal — to hide the lid — when everything inside had been closed from view. *I would have chosen warm-colored, mahogany wood rather than cold metal, but . . .*

Flanked on either end by tall standing lamps, the coffin seemed too fixed, too perfectly placed, as though situated to complete a scene. Fashioned with iridescent, opaque shades, the lamps, with subdued light, gave eerie illumination to the far end of the room. And except for the subject to which they offered quiet radiance, they would have been

unnecessary. They provided a focal point, though not a pleasant one for me.

But I had not expected this to be a pleasant setting.

Even during my most creative moments, I had not envisioned this scene; the thought had been too painful. There was something too deep and mysterious about this reality. I hadn't wanted to experience it; I had not been ready. But now it was being revealed, too suddenly, too completely. I wanted to retreat, but I knew no escape. *Grief, so firmly, had fastened its roots; and a stone was hung around my heart.*

What I had borne previously had dealt heavy blows to my waning courage. But I had only *imagined* how it would be; I didn't *know* how it would be. I hadn't wanted to know. Yet, I could not deny that sooner or later it must come to this. This was not a part that I was acting out; this was a part I was living. I was too aware, too conscious.

Inside the casket, wearing a peach-colored shroud trimmed in ivory lace and pearls, lay the frail figure of my mother. I was seeing her, but *not* seeing her.

According to Aunt Margaret, James Merritt had "performed a miracle," Robert told me. I didn't understand exactly what Robert was saying; nor at this point could I comprehend the precise meaning of Aunt Margaret's comment. Perhaps it was better that I did not. The obvious had been withheld from me, and for good reason. *They hadn't wanted me to know just how awful the last few weeks had been.*

I took a long look from the arched doorway. My mother lay still, in profile against the off-white lining of the casket. Nathan and Robert steadied me as we walked forward. The

scene was moving toward me, and I toward it. For a moment, I resisted the prodding of my son and brother. I was looking at something I did not want to see; and I didn't want them to be guiding me toward it. Someone dearer and more precious than many persons would ever know had been taken from me — had been taken from us all.

But Mama had not been afraid. *I* was the coward.

A few more steps forward, a three-quarter view of what lay before me, and then I was at her side. With cautious reluctance, I looked down at her slender hands, half-hidden under the folds of the long, lace cuffs; then slowly leftward until my eyes focused on her face. Then I looked above the casket and stared at the wall: the cream-colored wall — the *empty* wall which held my gaze — away from what I had no desire to see, what I could not *bear* to see.

For several moments, I felt suspended somewhere. I wanted to be removed from this place, relieved of this necessity. But regardless of where I went, ultimately this scene would return, and I would have to accept it. It may as well be now. Once more her face came into view. This time I let my eyes stay.

My mother actually looked good. The months of deterioration did not show. This must have been the "miracle" Aunt Margaret had mentioned. I had expected the worst, but that was how I viewed anything unpleasant; and I could not help it. My mother knew that, and had often told me that nothing is ever as bad as it first seems. But she had not been talking about herself, or this situation. Yet again I would be reaping the wisdom she had sown; again I would be acknowledging that she was right, even if I did not want to receive the truth gladly.

But my mother *did* look good. At her throat she wore her antique cameo of the Three Graces set in a heavy, yellow gold mounting, surrounded by ribbon swirls and delicately carved and engraved flowers in both silver and gold. Inherited from her paternal grandmother, this broach had been one of her favorite pieces of jewelry for as long as I could remember. *Even now, I recalled their names from ancient literature, as Mama had told me: Charm, Splendor, Joy. Details again.*

Mama's silver hair lay in soft waves, and was pulled back from her face and tied in a bun almost identical to one that she herself might have arranged. Her countenance looked peaceful, and almost smooth. The makeup was tastefully done, something my mother would have insisted upon, as she disdained anything more than subtle enhancement. I could almost hear her say: "Now, not too much; I've never worn a lot of makeup. And I don't want to look artificial." To my mother, restraint had been the greater part of beauty. Somehow the cosmetologist had known.

The funeral director was allowing us privacy. The doors to the viewing room closed almost too loudly, and I flinched against Robert's shoulder. He braced me with a trembling hand as Nathan and Bob stood on either side of me.

"Hello, Mama," I heard myself speaking in a hoarse whisper. I stroked her face and arm with a soft touch of my fingers, then bent to touch her cheek with my own. "I'm home now, Mama."

Somehow, I felt that she was smiling behind the serious expression she wore. Her face always lit up when I'd come home and say those words; and she would respond: "I see you are; and I am certainly glad."

I became aware of tears from somewhere. They were mine, but they seemed to come almost as much from relief as from grief. My mother's suffering was over — that was the relief; but she was *gone* — that was the grief. And my defenses were withdrawing. Inwardly, I heard myself saying: "I'm sorry I didn't get here sooner; I'm sorry about so many things." Then I heard sobs that came from deep within me, and Robert was asking if everything was to my "liking."

He indicated the casket and everything regarding Mama's appearance. He seemed to approach the subject with cold deliberation, but he had to ask the question. He had to be certain that I was satisfied.

I nodded my approval, but almost admitted that I might have preferred mahogany. But I pushed that selfish thought away, while my eyes were still fixed on Mama's face. I swallowed. "Could I be alone with her for a while?" Robert whispered in the affirmative and motioned for Nathan and Bob to follow him. Doors opened and closed as I still stood in front of the casket, my hand resting on my mother's shoulder.

I suddenly felt a strange calmness, much as when Mama would hold me when I was very, very young, presenting a mother's security and love without decided purpose. Her smile had always been eager on her lips, and she was naturally affectionate but had never been overly demonstrative. Such had not been her manner. Every gesture, every touch, every word of caring she expressed was a special one — never given so freely as to lose its value, yet never so reserved as to induce unrequited longing.

I knew that even now my mother would want me tranquil, relaxed, and conscious of all the finer things she had taught me; and, yes, just as conscious of her quiet caring. But she would not want me sad, nor despairing; she would want me strong and even happy that she had left the temporal realm. After all, she was "done with lesser things."

I could feel a communication with her, of former times and events, and even the most recent exchanges we'd had. This, her demise, her "release," as she might have called it, was the final resolution. All previous resolves were unimportant and paled in significance. I was positive that Aunt Margaret would later urge me to think of the happy times, the good memories we had of Mama — her favorite sister. Those memories were many.

* * * * * *

I did not know now, nor would I know for some time to come, just how unpleasantly Aunt Margaret viewed my "decision": the decision to withhold from my mother the medical remedies that she and Mama's other sisters thought appropriate. I saw Mama only as a mother's youngest son would see her; I tried to carry out her wishes, to respect her requests, to abide by promises I had made — to the very letter. I believed in my heart that that was what Mama wanted; I believed in my heart — and reasoned in my mind — that what I did, or did not do, was what was right for Mama. *She had made me promise.*

Aunt Margaret, Aunt Lucia, and Aunt Leela (who was next in age to Mama) saw my purpose as one clouded by emotion. Yet, Aunt Leela viewed my intentions as honorable, even if questionable. "Any purpose of his — any decision Sonny made —" she would acknowledge quietly, and only then if she were asked: ". . . was simply because he loved Eva *so much*."

Aunt Margaret and Aunt Lucia were not so easily convinced; they proved to be analytical and logical in their thinking, in their exercise of covenant keeping. "Sometimes, rules must be broken to produce a better end." A change of mind and heart regarding those "promises" might exact a certain measure of recovery, at least ". . . to make Eva feel better, to keep her from starving," as Aunt Margaret had expressed it so strongly. "You do not want to kill —" she had stopped short. *Kill? Surely Aunt Margaret had not meant to say what I thought I'd heard!*

Years would pass before Aunt Lucia and Aunt Margaret would teach their lesson through wills and deeds — not altogether without someone else's encouragement, some in the family would later suggest. *But why?* Aunt Leela would never speak openly of my decision nor appear to think any less of me. Indeed, at this moment, it never occurred to me that I had done anything exceedingly wrong, although I regretted Mama's insistence that I carry out her wishes. I was the obedient son. I was also the favored nephew. But that was now.

* * * * * *

In front of the casket I stood. It was as though lead held my feet in place; the sum total of all that I was kept me still, kept my mind and heart fixed on what lay before me. Memories engulfed my consciousness and tempered every feeling, every reasonable thought, every feasible idea. I was here; now I was finally with her. Certainly, I could not deny my sadness, nor would my mother require that. She would not want me to be untrue to myself in any way.

I could not help wanting her back. She had given me life at so great a cost, but had never spoken of that suffering

except as being worthwhile. Anything worth having, she would always say, was deserving of some price. "Anything of value possesses its own merit — just as beauty is its own excuse for being," she had paraphrased the literary saying. I knew she believed that.

And if I cried now, she'd understand that, too. "It takes a big man to cry," I'd heard her say. To her, there was no weakness in tears — unless those tears represented some frivolous reaction. But to deny one's feeling was wrong; and to my mother, the dismissal of *real emotion* did not constitute strength.

So, she would not think me weak to show feelings I could not hide, did not care to hide. She would simply accept me as "Sonny," insisting again that I need not try to be more or less than I was. I could not be dishonest at her back, nor to her face. Integrity was ingrained in her character, and she had reflected that toward us. Some of it, at least, had taken.

Looking at her face now, I was remembering so much. Her face had always been kind, even when she disciplined us. And that gentle face would ever remain in my memory; but more important would be the recollection of her supreme goodness. Her character, for all my scrutiny, had few detectable flaws at most; but she would never desire anyone's excessive lauding, and would be embarrassed to consider such. Though confident and dignified, she was nevertheless unassuming. Even toward the end, she had lived with all the dignity she could muster, but did so, it seemed, as a matter of course.

And as she lay before me now, she did not appear cold and lifeless. Even in this state she possessed a vibrance

all her own, at once simple and grand, owing, of course, to what she had been: thoroughly and indisputably genuine. No one could find guile in my mother. However hard one might have looked, there had *never* been any deceit to find. And certainly it occurred to me, as I looked at her face, her form, the apparent warmth effected by the peach-colored shroud, that other fortunate sons and daughters could identify with my feeling. *The Three Graces: Charm, Splendor, Joy. Mama had possessed these and numerous other virtues, but she would be embarrassed at my attribution. But, again, I could not help being myself.*

Some higher power had taken my father when I was seventeen, but had allowed me to keep my mother until I was past forty — and she, ninety. That thought alone should give me solace. It did, but not as much as I needed. I was human. Still, I felt a profound sense of gratitude that we'd been privileged to have known her, and to have loved her.

I caressed her cheek and hair and the soft fabric of her shroud, then the lace at her neck and hands — and finally, the cameo — feeling no shame at my devotion, nor considering myself any less a man. Then I leaned down once more to touch her face to mine, and I was all right for a moment.

A spontaneous whisper came from my lips: "I love you, Mama." She almost smiled. Many times during her illness, I had touched my cheek to her hair and had said with some humor, so as to bring her pleasure: "I love 'my mama'"; and she had always replied, though sometimes in a weak voice, "And I love 'my baby.'" Her affirmation never failed to solidify the truth; and the expression on her face at every instance made me know that I had done the appropriate thing.

If there were anything unmasculine about a son loving his mother and showing it, that didn't matter now. Certainly it had *never* mattered to me. I did not feel ashamed. I was glad to love her.

A knock on the door broke my reverie, and I became aware of someone tugging on my sleeve. Nathan had slipped in quietly and was standing beside me. I had not heard him speak.

"Are you ready, Daddy?" he repeated. "There are people waiting to see you."

Chapter 14

WAITING IN THE FOYER with the funeral director, my brother Robert, and his son Bob, were my mother's sisters.

The picture of elegance, Aunt Margaret initiated the greeting with her stately manner. She was straight and tall with a trim figure — and finely complexioned. Her make-up was impeccably applied with a hint of pink at the cheeks and a deeper color on her lips, and only a touch of mascara on her naturally dark lashes and brows, which enhanced her deep blue eyes to good advantage. Her expertly coiffed brown hair was neatly combed from a side part, and fell slightly below her ears, tapering to just above her wide, stand-up collar.

Appearing much younger than her seventy years, she was dressed in French blue and wore only one adornment — an exquisite diamond ring. Her hug was warm but unprolonged. In her opinion, affection was private and never given without real meaning, and even then to special people

only. Resisting many suitors, Aunt Margaret had never married; the only love of her life had been lost at sea during World War II.

I felt suspended, yet close enough to see, to notice, to remember. The stranglehold of grief, though loathe to let go, released me for just a while. For a few moments, I was winning the inner battle. I was observing again: details.

Aunt Lucia, as usual, wore an expensive and tastefully fashioned outfit with matching accessories — complete with kid gloves, and imported snakeskin bag and shoes: elaborate attire to be sure. Somehow I always noticed her splendid, high-fashion apparel, though she never made pretentious displays. This time, her silk ensemble was chocolate brown and creamy beige. Her short, silver-blonde hair was fashioned in loose curls, but away from her smooth forehead (allowing her widow's peak to show), and was flattering to her oval face, glowing skin, and pale blue eyes. She wore a minimum of makeup: lipstick in a light coral shade, and only the softest hue of mascara. She was porcelain-like in appearance; she had been a real beauty — and had traveled widely. Enormously intelligent and business-minded, Aunt Lucia had been quite successful in stocks and commodities.

Together with Aunt Margaret, she owned a large, L-shaped turn-of-the-century, Victorian-style home on Second Street — ornately decorated with porches, an elaborate portico-styled bay window, hand-carved moldings, and other effects — sitting on prime, street-front property, and situated on a huge, tree-shaded, landscaped lot: a home that one day I would inherit, they had said, along with household furnishings I had admired, plus treasures from the past, and funds.

At seventy-nine, Aunt Lucia was still stunning. She had around her neck the ever-present strand of deep-sea pearls given to her by her late husband, a noted psychologist: the author of six books and scores of articles, and professor emeritus of two state universities. On her ears, she wore the matching earrings: large pearls surrounded by tiny diamonds.

More sensitive than Aunt Margaret and more inclined to verbalize her sentiments, she hugged me for a long moment and kissed me lightly on the cheek, while commenting on how tall Nathan had grown and what a nice young man he was. She patted me on the back, softly cleared her throat, and said something about my jacket.

Childless as she was, Aunt Lucia accorded particular favor to me, whom she often referred to as "my favorite nephew" — as did Aunt Margaret. In conversation with friends and family — and oftentimes with mere acquaintances — she would add: "Dr. Clemmons and I had hoped to have a son just like Sonny. He is very special, you know. We don't forget those who are nice to us."

With that, she would pat me on the back, allowing her hand to rest there momentarily, as today: "Don't disappoint us, Sonny." Then she would smile and say: "We know you *won't*." She would then add, sometimes teasingly: "Neither do we forget the ones who *do* disappoint us." Her meaning was clear.

So overshadowed and smothered as I was by the blinding, numbing hand of grief, how could I notice and recall so much? My observant eye would not be closed; my acute memory would not be dulled — even now, when nothing else should matter. Someone had made me understand

that sometimes my mind was too active, my heart too tender, my spirit too troubled. "Beyond this realm, the circle may be unbroken; . . . someday we will meet on 'that beautiful shore'; but for now, accept that which cannot be changed."

Absent from the group was Aunt Trillis, who, seven years earlier, had died suddenly from a massive stroke. Were she here, she would have vied with Aunt Lucia in style and fashion, and no doubt would have worn a fur. Just above Aunt Lucia in age, she had worn heavier, but tastefully applied, makeup — even red nail polish at times — and would flash her very blue eyes at every turn. Having turned completely gray at the age of twenty-five, Aunt Trillis had snow-white hair by her early thirties and had never dyed it. I don't remember seeing her without white hair — and certainly never when it was not professionally styled, and lustrous. That is the way I remembered her today, as I saw her clearly in my mind.

Aunt Trillis had loved expensive jewelry, and owned a vast collection, but had worn it well — though not always sparingly. One ring on each hand was never enough — and always, there was a matching necklace and earrings, or an heirloom lavaliere. I remembered in particular an ornate, diamond bracelet-watch of white gold. When in her presence, on dress-up occasions, I would often ask her the time, just to be able to look at the watch. She would snap her eyes at me, tease me with a smile, extend her hand, and remark: "As if you really *needed* to know the time, Sonny." Then she would pat my arm, something she generally refrained from doing with others. Aunt Trillis's very cordial husband, Uncle Linton, had preceded her in death, and had left a noticeable void. When possible, they had gone everywhere together.

Interestingly, both Aunt Trillis and Uncle Linton had had a talent for horticulture: in particular, for raising African violets, which thrived under their touch. At one time, during my late teens, they owned an astonishing 5,000 plants of every variety and color. Their home had been a virtual greenhouse — violets everywhere — and Uncle Linton had added a windowed-in back porch just for displaying the innumerable plants, cuttings of which they often gave to interested friends and neighbors.

When Uncle Linton died, so did the violets — one by one — until, at the end, Aunt Trillis had a mere fifty remaining (the exact number with which they had begun their enterprise). She could never explain the reason for their dying; Aunt Trillis insisted that she had given them "the same care as before," to use her words. Not one to show much emotion, she would turn her head when someone asked her about the violets, and she would change the subject. Just before Uncle Linton died, a featured story about the violets — complete with several photographs — had been planned for an area newspaper and was ready for publication; but when a sudden heart attack took Uncle Linton, Aunt Trillis understandably asked the editor-publisher not to print the story.

Aunt Trillis and Uncle Linton's only child, Clarice, a registered nurse of noted proficiency, was joyful, happy — and had a musical laugh — but could be sternly serious when matters required. She had checked on Mama many times for me during this awful year, and had assured me by phone that everything possible (that "Aunt Eva will allow") was being done for her. Clarice told everyone that she thought of me as the brother she never had — and I was very fond of Clarice, considerate cousin that she was. Distance and time

might mar the relationship; but if so, I would never understand why.

Why was my weary soul, with its weight of care, calling forth so many conjectures, speculations? Why could I not govern the conscious thoughts that invaded every corner of my mind? Perhaps such remembrances helped lift the too-heavy burden that was crushing me, killing me.

I began to ease my way across the room, then paused for a moment. Again I found myself in the present.

Aunt Leela appeared somewhat more retiring than when I'd last seen her. She was sitting forward on one of the blue velvet sofas. Her genteel manner came from a natural quality that was continually with her; and though she had not been well, her calm, restrained attitude was inborn; it did not come from fatigue.

She waited for me to advance toward her. She was reserved and quiet, refined — dressed nicely but a little more conservatively than Aunt Margaret and Aunt Lucia. She wore a pale gray suit, a dark silver-gray blouse, and gray shoes — with a gray bag clutched at her side. In her hand she held a lace handkerchief — *just like Mama. . . .*

She appeared much like my mother in demeanor and hairstyle. Her graying, chestnut-colored hair shone in the light. Parted in the middle, it lay in soft finger waves, and was tied in a braided figure eight at the back of her head. Her makeup consisted of the palest, most natural shade of pink lipstick — nothing more. Her eyes, now with noticeable redness, were hazel — with specks of green and yellow, which had afforded her many admiring glances when a young woman.

At eighty-six, and ten years a widow, she was striking: neat, slender, smooth of skin. She and my mother had been close, so much alike in looks, carriage, and deportment; always correct in manner, polished in appearance, immaculately dressed.

I walked to where Aunt Leela was sitting, bent down to receive her hug. "I'm glad to see you, Sonny." Her voice was gentle, kind; she had always been soft-spoken. Aunt Leela was very fond of me, even if from afar, and had rewarded my every visit home with her best angel food cake. This time would be no different. It was her way of communicating affection that her breeding would not allow her to express directly.

Her son, Richard, was on her arm. He drove for Aunt Leela since his retirement (and especially since Uncle Noah had died), and took her wherever she wanted or needed to go. He extended his big hand, and with a large smile made a witty comment about my "getting rich in Texas."

He asked Bob: "Can't you help your Uncle Sonny figure out a way to spend all that money?" Bob said that he would be glad to try. When Richard asked Nathan where he'd gotten that red hair and beard, Nathan reminded him that "Grandmother Eva's hair" had been "reddish in color."

With her characteristic authority, Aunt Margaret broke through the light conversation and became serious. "How do you think your mother looks, Sonny?"

"Very nice," I answered. She nodded, then turned to Nathan.

"And you, son, how do *you* think your grandmother looks?"

"She looks just like she's asleep, Aunt Margaret." Nathan's sincerity countermanded whatever triteness his response might have contained. He then turned and nodded toward a large standing wreath of pink and white flowers bearing the word "Sister" on its gold-and-pink-colored ribbon. "The flowers are beautiful, Aunt Margaret." I concurred, and all three aunts seemed pleased.

Aunt Margaret lifted a finger ever so slightly toward the funeral director and spoke to me directly, with a nod in Robert's direction. "Didn't I tell you that James Merritt had performed a miracle?" Then, as though to explain to me: "She looks so much better than she did the last few weeks, Sonny. She had been through so much. I am really quite glad that you didn't have to see her that way."

I felt emotion welling up again from inside, but I refused to allow it to break free. "I know, Aunt Margaret — and I'm very grateful that he was able to do such a good job." Then to James: "Thank you for your excellence."

He smiled. "I'm glad you're satisfied, Sonny. I wanted to do my very best for you."

Nathan urged me to take a closer look at the flowers my aunts had given, as well as the numerous other arrangements bearing names of relatives and friends. Other deliveries were being put in place even during our conversation, and James would point out especially attractive ones for me to notice. Without care or design, the delivery boys stood the wreaths in any empty space, as though expecting the funeral home to arrange the flowers properly.

Something within me wanted to organize the flowers, to harmonize them according to color, height, and size;

but I resisted; I should not worry about this matter. One of James Merritt's experienced assistants would position the flowers later — without need of *my* supervision.

My aunts made a few parting remarks to each of us. Aunt Margaret paused in mid-smile, and with an extremely solemn expression looked directly at me for a minute. She took a step toward me as if she intended to say another private word or two, but did not. She then turned away, joined the others, and was gone.

Robert suggested that we go to Mama's for lunch where other family members and friends would be waiting. It was already eleven o'clock.

I turned for one more brief look at Mama, instinctively signed the register, and walked out into the sunlight with Robert, Nathan, and Bob following. James Merritt waited until we were seated in the car and were driving off before he closed the big doors.

Chapter 15

AS WE APPROACHED MY MOTHER'S HOUSE, I could see the figure of Marvin, Priscilla's husband, sitting in the porch swing. His car was parked near the walk; I knew that he'd had to help Priscilla into the house. I knew how immensely distraught she must be, for Robert and the others had told me that she had taken Mama's death badly; and I knew Priscilla. She would keep her grief inside as much as possible, but she would hurt so deeply that she would cause herself unmerciful agony. That was her way.

As we walked up the steps, Marvin approached me with an outstretched hand. He raised and shrugged his shoulders to adjust the fit of his blue-and-brown plaid jacket, and offered me a brief hug.

"Hello, Sonny. Sure am sorry about your mother — such a fine woman."

Then, in his Harker's Island, Cockney-sounding accent, with a quiet tone of very obvious concern: "Priscilla

says that she's not even going to be able to look at Miss Eva. I can't reason with her, but maybe you can."

"I'll talk to her, Marvin."

Inside the house, down the carpeted, mirror-laden hall, and past its various other contents and appointments (which this time I ignored) — past a myriad of floral arrangements, past the registry stand, past numerous persons sitting in adjoining rooms and sections of the hallway, a turn to the left into the sitting room; and I found Priscilla sitting in the northeast corner. She was isolating herself from all family members and friends.

The lamp atop the mahogany table next to her was noticeably off, though several other lamps in the room emitted subdued, yellow light — effecting warmth and hospitality, even during this saddest of times. The light of day also shone through the open curtains and blinds.

I knew that Priscilla had switched off the lamp for added privacy. She preferred a darkened corner when troubled — although she would never choose total darkness, as it had always frightened her. Mama's picture above the mantel, on the west wall across from Priscilla, seemed to look down upon her as if to soften her grief. But Priscilla appeared oblivious even to my presence.

She was sitting motionless in the rose-colored armchair, eyes cast downward toward the tweed-patterned carpet. She wore brown shoes with low heels, her slender feet drawn close together, one slightly in front of the other, in keeping with her usual poise. Her skirt, pulled tightly around her legs, covered her knees. She epitomized modesty.

Directly under her feet lay a fringe-bordered, rose-and-blue area rug — one she had generally admired. She had frequently sat in this spot when visiting Mama, and invariably commented on the rug: its colors and how wonderfully they were organized in the intricate design. She and I had shared our admiration regarding this and various other household appointments, on other, more pleasant, occasions. That was one way we related: our manner and subject of conversation.

Today, for Priscilla, the rug did not matter; nor did anything else of a material nature. Nothing really appeared "pretty" today. I well understood. Shifting her gaze but a fraction, Priscilla looked away from where she sat. She stared aimlessly at a cut-glass vase of white cushion mums that had been placed on a marble-top table in the center of the room — seeing, without seeing. Then, again she cast her eyes downward toward the tweed-patterned carpet. She said nothing.

Her gray hair, which once had been a rich auburn and always expertly arranged, was now pulled back from her forehead in a severe style, with a tight twist at the back. She appeared older than her sixty years, but with good cause. She was not well; had not been well for as long as I had known her.

Today, she had on a shirt-waisted brown-and-black dress, trimmed in beige. She wore no jewelry, not even her watch or wedding rings. They made her nervous, she said, when they shifted out of position on her arm or fingers; and, today, she was not wearing her glasses. She wore not even a speck of makeup; she was pale; her lips looked unnaturally purple. This pallor was everpresent, fixed; and had been so for thirty years.

Kneeling in front of her, I pried her white hands apart and attempted to penetrate her trance-like posture. "Priscilla,

everyone says that Mama looks so much better now — more like she used to look. I was able to look at her; surely *you* can. I'll go with you if you want me to — but you *should* see her. I think it'll make you feel a lot better. Nathan will take us." Nathan, who a few moments earlier had quietly entered the room, assured her in the affirmative as I motioned toward him. He was standing beside me, leaning forward, with one hand on my shoulder.

Priscilla trembled slightly, squeezed my hand, and shook her head. "I just can't, Sonny — not now. Maybe later." Then she began to cry softly, as though resigned to permanent grief. She had already pulled apart several Kleenex tissues which lay beside her in the chair.

Of the five brothers and sisters, Priscilla's temperament was more like my own. We both took matters quite seriously — perhaps too seriously at times. Yet, this experience was something we'd never before encountered. The only other time we had felt a similar helplessness was when our father had died. As a teenager, I had not been ready — did not know how — to deal with death; and Priscilla had been away and had not arrived home in time to see Daddy alive, though he had asked for her.

I knew now how she had felt then, and she surely knew the inner burden that pulled at me. She did not communicate this understanding verbally, but I could sense what she wanted to say.

I had been very close to this sister over the years and could identify with her excessive grief. Inclined to give in to her own suffering, she nevertheless demonstrated a resilience I envied. I had seen her snap back from many a trauma; but this one was extremely difficult for her. Poor health had prevented her doing a lot for Mama, though she had tried; and she'd hated that. She had wanted so much to be able to sit long hours with Mama and wait on her, much as Rebecca Ann and Francine had done.

She must have been struggling with those regrets now, in addition to Mama's passing, so her pain was logical, and understandable. Yet, I wanted her to break away from herself for a moment; I wanted her to see Mama, so she might find some relief.

But Priscilla, like our mother, would not be persuaded to do what she did not want to do. I urged her again: "Priscilla, please — go with me to see Mama. It will make you feel better — it did me."

She pulled her beige sweater tighter around her shoulders. "I said, '*No,*' Sonny. I just *can't.* I feel so very sick." She looked up at me, almost in desperation it seemed, and sighed. I nodded, patted her shoulder, and left her alone.

Her resolve would not be broken. She would never see our mother's face again. She would remember her the way she had looked the day before she died.

Voices of other relatives in the room and throughout the house distracted us from our moment of sharing. Dee was prompting us to eat. I became aware of the distinctive scent of baked ham among other pleasant fragrances emanating from the far end of the house. Again I could almost see Mama, or feel her presence — as she, and whoever happened to be helping her, would come from the kitchen and dining room, bringing with them the smell of the wonderful food they had prepared — with Mama herself calling us to "dinner." Meals around Mama's table were little less than feasts in abundance and flavor.

This time, though, the voice was Rebecca Ann's, not Mama's. "Sonny, come on, now, you need to eat something." Being the eldest, she was standing in for Mama, and speaking directly to me. Like the proverbial mother hen, she had taken me under her wing. She sometimes had a tendency to take control, but someone had to in situations like this. And Rebecca Ann did it well.

Other family members were urging everyone else toward the kitchen and dining areas, where food was being served buffet-style. Hope asked Francine to join her. Francine coaxed Priscilla, but to no avail. Francine herself would not eat until Priscilla decided that she could. *There would be a long wait.*

Chapter 16

IN THE KITCHEN, JOSEPH WAS STANDING BY THE SINK, in front of the double windows, looking out over the barren fields toward the dense forest beyond. He was holding a cup of coffee absentmindedly in one hand while he puffed on a cigarette. A full ashtray of half-smoked cigarettes sat before him in the sink; a crushed package lay on the blue-and-mauve counter.

I knew that he had smoked a lot already and would smoke many more cigarettes as the day wore on. I had cautioned him about heavy smoking, as had other family members; but his habit seemed more like a nervous response than desire for the taste of tobacco. A smudge of fallen ashes lay on the sleeve of his brown leather jacket; he neither noticed, nor seemed to care.

Releasing the cup momentarily, he rubbed his forehead with his right hand, then ran his fingers over his red-brown hair, smoothing a wayward lock back into place. This,

too, was a habit, not vanity. But Joseph liked his hair slicked back — neat; he was never without a comb, though this time the comb stayed wherever it was. He drew in a breath, lay the cigarette on the side of the ashtray, then shifted his weight to his left foot, and braced himself now with both hands on the edge of the sink.

Tonight would be bad on Joseph, and I didn't know what tomorrow might bring for him. However strong, he could not endure much suffering on the part of others; and death, to him, was so final that no amount of words could lift him from his sullen mood.

Relatives in the kitchen and dining area, and some who had ventured through the open door to the screened-in-and-windowed porch, occasionally spoke a word to him, offering him plates of food and more coffee. He seemed to hear without hearing, spoke his thanks as a matter of fact, and continued to stare with gray eyes toward the woods, while lighting another cigarette. The one waiting in the ashtray was still burning, and sent swirls of smoke toward the blue-mauve ceiling; but Joseph did not notice.

He drew a heavy sigh. "Mama used to walk there among the pines," I heard him say. He was not speaking to anyone in particular, just remembering.

"When she was well, and when she was certain that no one was watching, she would even do a slow run down the path and back during the late afternoons and early mornings — just for the exercise. I can well remember when Cleo or Brandy would run along with her, barking all the way there and back. A half mile at least — and Mama did that nearly every day when the weather wasn't bad. So dignified, but still she'd run slow-like for the exercise."

Aware of my presence, he turned to look at me, then back toward the woods. "You remember, Sonny?" He knew that I did.

I stepped up beside him, placed my hand on his arm to show him that I understood, and then I moved aside to give him breathing room. He needed space; he had always needed personal space and would allow few people, even close relatives, to share that space. His current, favorite girlfriend, Dorcas (one of several during the past year), sat alone in one of the guest bedrooms. She knew when not to bother him. She had been crying; I understood why.

I thought I detected a faint odor on Joseph's breath that I did not like, but I would not attempt to chastise. I was surely not without fault, and I knew that he had been through a lot lately. To his own way of thinking, he had the right to handle his concern and grief in his own manner, even if it wouldn't have pleased our mother. But no one could question his love for her. Perhaps seeing her skin tear had been too much for him. I hoped that when all matters were settled, he would be himself again — if ever he might.

What had happened this past Wednesday night, two nights before Mama died, had left Joseph at once anxious and apathetic; indifferent, strange. He hardly knew where he was or what he was doing. Reality was too real; pain was too painful; dying was too inevitable. He had to have his escape. He would choose it where best he might find it. What had happened three nights ago had been too much. . . .

* * * * * *

It was just after supper last Wednesday. " 'Scuse me, y'all." Dee stood in the doorway of the living room — a room

— 111 —

seldom used now except for Sunday guests, or when the minister would call, or when there was an overflow crowd of family and friends in the house, as now.

"Joseph, would y'min' comin' in heah fo'a minute, please?" She indicated Mama's room with a tilt of her head. "Need y'help with yo' mothah — need y' t' help 'Beck' an'me t'mov'a ovah on t' othah side. I know she's ti'ed a'lyin' this way; been like this fo' two 'ouwahs o' moah. She dutt'n look comfo'ble t'me."

Extending quiet cordialities and apologies to "the company," the several visitors in the living room, Joseph rose quickly from the gold brocaded side chair, and hastened across the hall to where Dee and Rebecca Ann were tending to Mama. Rebecca Ann had momentarily gone into her bedroom adjoining Mama's room, where, from Mama's cedar chest, she was getting an afghan throw for Mama's feet. The room was not cold, but Mama had indicated that her feet were. So "Beck," always alert, always quick to do whatever needed doing, was just returning with the green-and-red knitted throw in her hands as Joseph approached the foot of Mama's bed.

"How do we do this?" Joseph wanted to be certain that when they turned Mama, they would cause no more discomfort for her than necessary. He had asked the question a hundred or more times before, never trusting that he had remembered the procedure; and thinking that perhaps some modification of the method might produce less distress, less agony for Mama and also for himself.

The immensely swollen leg was tender, sore, raw in places — had begun taking on a blackish tone — and was never free of intense pain, so repositioning Mama, however

tenderly, never failed to hurt her, to bring uncharacteristic groans and "Oh, oh" from her lips. The slightest movement brought on unbearable spasms that came involuntarily, and now almost in regular intervals of no more than a few minutes apart. The doctors had said that these were "normal; to be expected."

Every time he was asked to assist in this manner, Joseph dreaded the request, the act, and especially the result (the moans, the cries) — though he well knew the necessity of keeping Mama turned, not only for comfort, but also to prevent pressure points from causing sores. Still, he could barely stand it. He became ghastly white each time Mama groaned, but he would smile and say a cheerful word to her; this was all he knew to do. His smile never lasted long.

The sounds of pain from our mother sickened Joseph; but no one else in the family this night, at this precise moment, was available to help. Robert was at work, and the older grandsons were otherwise occupied. None of the male neighbors or family members in the living room had experience in this chore, so Joseph was the only one convenient at the moment; and the always-considerate Rebecca Ann knew that Mama would prefer not to have a neighbor assist in this personal task for her.

Mama had indicated that her present position on the bed was uncomfortable for her — not verbally, but by the expression on her face. Both Dee and Rebecca Ann had noticed and knew the signs.

Mama had grown so much weaker, totally unable to help move herself, unable to push up onto her elbows, to assist in any way. Even lifting her head on her own was now hardly possible.

She had worsened to the degree that now she was almost dead weight, totally helpless; almost listless; weak of voice, weaker still of body; almost lacking even in spirit. Her eyes hardly ever registered any joy; she now kept them closed most of the time, but would open them when someone spoke to her, asked a question, or needed clarification about something. So weak now, she saved her voice when she could, and nodded or shook her head, according to the response needed.

Joseph was more than willing to do anything for our mother, but he always dreaded the inevitable sounds that turning her brought forth — foreign sounds from our mother's lips, sounds all of us were unaccustomed to hearing: tormenting sounds. They nearly killed him.

Dee motioned for him to take Mama by the shoulders and left arm, to slide his right hand and arm under her back, and to lift her when she gave the word, while holding on to Mama's left arm with his left hand. Dee herself, standing across from Joseph, would slide Mama toward the center of the bed as Joseph pulled Mama closer to himself and then pushed her over as he had so often in the past. Rebecca Ann would lift both of Mama's legs at the same time, careful that the pillows between them remained in place, to soften the effect of turning, to avoid their striking and rubbing against each other during the procedure.

Everything seemed too methodical to Joseph, but had been deemed appropriate, even necessary, for this most unpleasant of duties. He sometimes was forced to close his eyes.

"Now; when I say 'Go,' let's all mov'a at t'same time," Dee was instructing. "Okay, now; go."

Suddenly, a startling scream from Mama. The left arm that Joseph was gripping felt slippery; at once dry and damp. Aghast, Joseph moaned, became ill; lay Mama back into position against the pillow and rushed from the room and down the hall — destroying a porcelain figurine in his haste — gagging, until reaching the lighted porch and grabbing the banister, he expelled from his stomach what would not stay down.

Rebecca Ann and Dee eased Mama back down into position and craned their heads to see what had so violently affected Joseph. They knew in their hearts what had happened. The flesh lay open, with pinkish-red and yellow liquid oozing from the torn arm. The dry skin hung in shreds; the pink-white flesh shone clearly, and part of Mama's upper arm was torn to the bone in a gaping wound. Her left shoulder blade protruded through the skin; the dampness on the back of the blue-and-pink gown told the story.

They had noticed small irritations before, and very tiny cuts, along with numerous blue-black bruises on Mama's skin: dermal hemorrhaging, even with the gentlest handling. What they had already observed sickened even Dee and Rebecca Ann, who regularly saw in Mama's deterioration things they had shared only with the doctors — and occasionally with the nurses who also were alert to these changes. But what they saw now . . .

Mama was groaning — low-pitched, guttural cries were coming from her vocal cords: sounds none of them had ever heard from our mother. Several visitors across the hall, on hearing the commotion, had rushed to Mama's room.

Rebecca Ann called out for towels, shouted for someone to call the doctors and tell them what had happened, to

call Robert and Francine and Priscilla, to call the preacher, to bring water, ice; to hand her lotion, ointment, bandages from the side table while she and Dee held on to Mama's quivering body. Both she and Dee were horrified, but did by rote what they knew to do, or what they thought they ought to do.

Applying cool cloths to the wounds, and trying her best to close them, Dee spoke to Mama as gently as she knew how, while Rebecca Ann bent her face to Mama's, fingered her hair in place, and apologized for hurting her. "The doctor will be here soon, Mama, and we'll get you something for the pain. Lord knows, I wish this had not happened. I'm sorry, Mama — so sorry, so very sorry." She blinked back the tears that came, kissed Mama again and again on the forehead.

Mama's eyes had blared open with the horrible suffering, the piercing torture, then closed against even the filtered light from the table lamps. She shuddered in extreme pain, intolerable pain; continued to breathe heavily in short, shallow breaths; moaned every time she exhaled, each sound growing weaker, less discernable. She then, mercifully, lost consciousness and lay completely still.

Joseph, regaining what little composure he could gather, rushed back into the dimly lit room. Seeing what he could not bear to see, though Dee and Rebecca Ann had covered the wounds, he wailed: "Oh, Mama!" It was unlike him to utter anything so vocal, so helpless, so demonstrative. He then began his animal-like vigil: walking back and forth down the long, wide hall like the proverbial caged cat. He only paused now and then to look in on Mama as Rebecca Ann, Dee, and a few family friends stood by, doing whatever they knew to do, while waiting for the doctor.

The immense pain had caused Mama to soil herself; and Rebecca Ann and Dee, with the help of two neighbor women from the adjoining room, were changing the bedclothes and Mama's gown and using lukewarm water and the mildest soap and lotion to clean her. The very idea would have been too embarrassing for Mama were she conscious; but this attention was vitally necessary, though grievous for Rebecca Ann in particular.

Rushing from the living room, where she had been sitting with the other "company," Hazel Lawton, an immensely devout Pentecostal Christian neighbor and long-time friend, with Bible in hand, immediately fell to her knees at the foot of Mama's bed — and began praying fervently in English and in a tongue unknown to the others present. There was no doubting her sincerity.

Unable to contain his impatience, and without thinking about what he was saying and not really caring, Joseph vented a loud, direct unction from his heart and mind: "Damn it all, what in the *hell* is keeping the doctor?"

The minutes they waited became proverbial hours — like so many other short periods of time they all had known during this travail. When Dr. Jackson finally arrived and had examined Mama, he drew everyone aside, deep into the lighted hall, away from where Mama lay still on the bed.

"I cannot sew up the wounds. Her skin will not hold the stitches. I have filled the gashes with antibiotic ointment. That's all I can do at the moment."

He then informed them pointedly but in gentle words that nothing more could be done, except to take Mama to the hospital, to give her whatever medical treatment was

available there — and to insert a feeding tube to rehydrate and nourish her, in an effort to "bring her back."

"She will regain consciousness from time to time," he assured, "but she is in such horrible agony, I don't know how much more she can stand." Then, back in Mama's room, and to Rebecca Ann and Dee, he pointed out the items he had brought, speaking in a low tone: "Apply this ointment sparingly with gauze dipped in cool, sterile water. Keep the wounds clean and closed, and bandage them every few hours with ointment-soaked bandages, overlapping those with dry bandages, attaching them with non-stick surgical tape. I'm going to call one of the nurses to come out here to help you."

Then directly to Rebecca Ann and Joseph, and in a whisper: "All of you children need to get together as soon as you can — tomorrow at the latest — and make a *definite* decision. Come to my office at ten in the morning, so everybody can get a clear understanding of what will take place — and don't let Priscilla put you off. I know her health isn't good and she is liable to be indecisive, but we *cannot* delay. Be sure she gets there!

"It will be best to have your lawyer draw up papers — for all to sign . . . have Robert get in touch with me as soon as he comes home . . . someone in the family can serve as proxy for Sonny with his consent . . . document everything, in the event something happens later to bring your actions into question . . . majority rules in these matters, but if all do not agree, well . . ."

Hearing all this talk, the usually calm Rebecca Ann began to fidget, but kept her composure. Joseph was shifting his weight from one foot to the other; he could not stand

much more of this monologue. The doctor said a few more words that escaped Rebecca Ann — all that he was saying was too much to take in at the moment. She was thinking about the conversation she had had with her "baby brother" last month, as I had boarded the plane for Texas, and had made my strong assertion regarding Mama's care.

As the doctor gave Mama a shot in her hip to ward off infection and another one for the pain, he offered more advice, and this time loudly: "Somebody *needs* to call Sonny, but you will have to decide *when*. He's bound to take this very —" The doctor stopped short. Then a soft word of warning: "Any time you touch Miss Eva now, you may see her skin tear further. Sorry. It can't be helped; just do the best you can."

Shaking his head in disbelief, Dr. Jackson could not hide his own emotion. Over the many months he had cared for Mama, he had grown close to "this lovable but stubborn, old woman."

"The flesh tore from her bones because of dehydration — almost total dehydration. I've never seen anyone so dehydrated and still be able . . ." He stopped, shook his head again; gave a few more instructions and was leaving. "Call me if you need me. Either Dr. Mallison or I will get here as soon as possible; but something must be done. She really needs to go to the hospital. Hardly any fluid at all left in her body; and unless we can get a feeding tube in her or give her glucose . . . don't know if we can even find a vein. Something must be done — and quickly!" With that, he shook his head, and was gone.

When Joseph heard this pronouncement, compounded by everything else the doctor had said and what he himself was feeling, he jumped into his red Ford truck and was off — off to find his "escape." So quickly did he exit the driveway — and without headlights — that he almost ran into the car driven by the minister from Mama's church. The Rev. Nigel Latrick, from Bethany Baptist, slammed on his brakes to avoid the collision. He recognized Joseph's red truck but had never seen Joseph so agitated, so careless. At that moment, Joseph could not have cared less what the minister thought.

Sadly, the time would come when Joseph would totally disregard all public favor — and the opinion of family and friends. But that eventuality could not, at this moment, be anticipated. That realization would come later, and to everyone's dismay; for in most circumstances, Joseph was one of the more dignified of Mama's children.

Something too terrible to explain, or to understand, had happened to Joseph Wednesday night.

* * * * * *

The real Joseph, though certainly no paragon of virtue, exhibited many fine qualities. Having no children of his own, this very caring brother doted on nephews and nieces, always remembering them with gifts at Christmastime, and lavishing attention on them whenever any one or several were in his presence. He might not express himself lovingly in a verbal manner, but he would not deny a reasonable request from the children, nor withhold a treat, toy, or game within his power to purchase or acquire. The nieces and nephews all looked forward to seeing "Uncle Joseph" and spending time with him.

He would take them for rides on his saddle horses, in his carriages or carts, in his truck, or on one of his John Deere tractors. He would take them to playgrounds or parks, where, like them, he would laugh and have all manner of fun until they dropped from fatigue. Then he would take them to get ice cream, candy, or a cold drink. He spoiled them; that was his way. He never seemed happier than when he had time with his nieces and nephews. He had especially catered to Nathan when Nathan's mother and I had chosen our separate paths. And Nathan was understandably partial to his Uncle Joseph, who called him "Nay."

Perhaps the most generous of Mama's children, Joseph was also the quickest of temper. Few people crossed his path when he was angry, but few there were also who had not received great accommodation from him. If someone needed transportation or assistance of any kind, Joseph was generally the first to be called and the first to respond.

Both he and Robert had been good brothers to me. While Robert was talkative and socially aggressive, Joseph was quieter and more prone toward somber moods. No one really knew exactly what he was thinking. Although thoroughly comfortable with children and animals, when in the company of adult persons (even close family) he would stiffen up, become quiet, distant. He rarely shared his inner feelings and would try to shrug off difficulties that were beyond easy handling. Sometimes he was successful; sometimes not.

He certainly could not shrug off Mama's death. Now — today — Sunday noon — in the kitchen, Mama's death was as close as it could be — *too close.*

Looking around, Joseph leaned against the sink and motioned for me to come nearer. "You know we're to meet at the funeral home tonight from seven until nine, to receive friends and relatives who wish to pay respects?"

I nodded. "Yes. Robert told me."

He looked at me for a long moment as though he wanted to tell me something. Then, as though thinking better of it, he turned abruptly toward the window and continued his gazing. He dismissed me with a jerk of his head.

As I left, I heard him whisper again: "She used to walk there."

Chapter 17

SUNDAY NIGHT: SIX-FORTY-FIVE, and already the parking lot was full. Cousins and other relatives — and many friends I hadn't seen in years — were standing on the brick porch. The well-lighted parking lot and hanging lamps on the porch provided a good view of people walking in and out of the funeral parlor, and others who were congregating in the yard around the vehicles.

Robert pulled his long, black car into a reserved parking space near the door, so I wouldn't have far to walk. He was hoping to save me as much as possible from some of the conversation I'd have to make with those waiting in the yard. However appreciative I was of condolences, responding to them was difficult; and Robert knew that I needed to conserve my strength.

Emotions were at the brink and almost overflowing for all of us; and as my mother's youngest, I would receive many gestures of kindness which would intensify the relentless

surging within. Many close relatives on both sides of the family had not had the occasion to speak to me, and would attempt to do so now.

That was the way things were; and undeniable pain would accompany every "thank-you" I would express.

At the steps, I was greeted by some relatives I hardly knew. Some of these were cousins of my mother, many near her age, but none so old. Most of Mama's contemporaries had preceded her in death. And many of the remaining ones who were able to come for this formal viewing knew me only as "Joe and Eva's baby," and spoke to me in this manner. Others who knew me better called me by name and acknowledged how terrible it must have been for me to come home under these circumstances.

Robert politely ushered me away from such well-intentioned persons and their comments. The sympathy was accepted with gratitude, but he did not want matters for me to be worse than they already were. When an emotional cousin fell on my shoulder in tears because of "Aunt Eva's much suffering," Robert and Nathan pulled me away, apologizing for being in a hurry to get me inside where I could be seated.

The thick of people inside the vestibule and waiting room made finding a seat quite difficult, and Robert shouldered his way through with many apologies, and finally guided me to a couch near the casket. He spoke over his shoulder several times to persons wanting to pay immediate respects. *What a crowded night it was becoming; what a crowded life, . . .*

I felt dizzy; the air inside the room seemed too close. Robert told me to take several deep breaths and to lean back on the couch. Nathan was a permanent fixture at my side and held my arm. My nephew Bob went to get me a cup of water.

I heard a whole orchestra of voices in the viewing room. Faces and bodies approached me. They had their say and I nodded my appreciation, or spoke whatever words I could. I somehow felt lifted above the scene, yet pulled back down to its stark reality.

My mother was lying in a coffin close by. Death was no visitor; death had come to stay. *The death angel had done his bidding: had come, had gone, had taken . . .*

Arms wound around my neck, hands were shaking mine, kisses were being placed on my cheek. Quiet words were being spoken by persons who leaned forward toward me.

Suddenly I was standing. Someone was saying something in concert with others. "Your mother surely looks good, Sonny. I know you're glad she looks so well. When did you get home? Did you arrive in time to see her — *alive*?" These and other questions and comments came, as were expected. I answered as well as I could, trying to smile whenever possible, and always thanking everyone. Comments came from many directions at once, above the tempered roar of the crowd.

"She doesn't look like the same Eva," I heard someone saying. "Why, I would hardly have recognized her!"

Someone else was speaking: "Before Sonny came along she was wonderfully beautiful, but she really went downhill fast after he was born. She almost died carrying him, you remember — and when Sonny was born, well, the doctors thought sure Eva wouldn't make it." *As if giving birth to me had caused her ruin.*

The woman making the remarks — a thin woman wearing very thick glasses — had not seen me standing behind her, and on her right. Her husband quickly drew her aside, whispered something in her ear, and I heard the woman exclaim, "Oh, I'm so sorry — I didn't know he was that close! Let me apologize to him." She looked over her shoulder but could not find me, as others had approached. I knew she had not meant to be so blunt, so harsh.

"Why, I would hardly have recognized Eva," another woman repeated. "Don't suppose I expected her to look so old — can't get over how much she has changed . . . remember how breathtakingly beautiful she looked at her and Joe's wedding that first Sunday in May 1918 . . . a high-noon ceremony at Reedy Branch . . . never saw such a crowd . . . of course, I was just a teenager, but I recall it so well . . . Joe broke his arm handcranking the car that day . . . he had to report to the Armed Forces the next day for the War in Europe . . . really, she just doesn't look like the *same* Eva." It was true. The years had drawn heavily on my mother's former beauty; and the last several months of her life had taken a great toll. It had been decades since many of her acquaintances had seen her, and it was natural for them to observe an enormous difference in her appearance.

But time and illness had not left my mother plain, though certainly she was not so attractive as many had remembered.

And some honest, outspoken individuals, like the one who had just spoken, were overheard to mention this fact to each other, if not to us. Still, there were those who maintained that considering what she had gone through, "Eva certainly looked good for her age." And she did. *Still, I could not relate totally, for Mama, though attractive, had always appeared somewhat old to me; she was well past her prime when I came along.*

More people were touching my arm, or shoulder, or patting my back, or shaking my hand, as they issued warm remarks regarding this occurrence. Many inquired as to my new location, what I was doing in the "big state of Texas," wanting to know why I had left Bayden, and if I shouldn't be coming back to live nearer my relatives. "Don't you know that everybody who loves you lives here?"

I could not answer all the questions, nor was that expected. Many of those who spoke to me were making polite conversation, as though to make matters better for me — to take my mind off the casket.

My brothers and sisters were receiving similar attention as that given me, as were my aunts and other close family members. Priscilla was conspicuously absent. Robert had to explain that she was not well and was taking the death very badly. Inquiries regarding Priscilla brought empathy and remembrances of the trauma she had suffered as a young woman, when she had been "one of the prettiest girls around, with that shoulder-length auburn hair and creamy skin."

An elderly woman, sitting by one of the marble pedestals near the casket, related in a high-pitched voice details of forty-five years ago. "Why, I don't believe Priscilla was more than sixteen when it happened." And others were adding to her recollection, agreeing or clarifying.

"I remember the trial — how she had to get on the stand and tell about how he was under her bed — and how she reached down to pull up the covers — and put her hand on his head — and she screamed for her mother and daddy. Well, it's just a wonder that it didn't cause her more harm

— such a pity for that to happen to such a pretty young girl. Guess that man is still in prison — no, I believe — yes, I heard that Joe signed for him to get out before he passed away — understand that Priscilla was at Joe and Eva's when the warden and the fellow's mother came to see Joe about agreeing for him to be released — didn't I hear that the woman used to help Eva with her children — and didn't the fellow work for Joe some, on the farms? Heard he had been a trusted worker. *Trusted indeed!*

"Well, anyway, the warden told Joe that the fellow had been such a model prisoner and had been so young when it had all happened — believe he was just a little older than Priscilla — well, since by some miracle Priscilla didn't really get hurt physically, thought it would be fair for him to get out — seems he had served about fourteen years — maybe more." A heavyset man was nodding his agreement.

"Joe told me that Priscilla never got over what happened to her — some people don't realize what that kind of thing can do to your nerves. And I'd heard Eva say that Joe never got over it, either — couldn't stand for something like that to happen to his daughter. 'Course, Eva never said much about her own feelings, but I knew she thought about it a lot, too.

"Some of the neighbors wanted to 'string the boy up,' I heard, but Joe would have nothing to do with anything illegal, though they told him to 'just speak the word, and he'll be dead meat by morning.'"

She then added quickly: "Sonny was just a baby when all that happened. . . ."

I could not believe the conversation: so harsh, so blatantly honest, so seemingly cruel — and from genteel, caring

Southern folk who were easygoing, kind, considerate; never hateful.

The woman doing the speaking adjusted her glasses, looked at me through bifocals, then turned to look at my mother. She whispered something to the blonde girl at her side, turned again to look in my direction, and resumed her talking to the others in the group. "I heard that everyone in the family has checked under their beds — every night — ever since that boy got in the house that way. Don't know that I blame them. I always felt a little uneasy myself after it happened and they found out who it was. And he acted like such a nice boy . . . shows you never know who you can trust."

Everyone was talking at once, yet in hushed tones. I somehow felt glad that Priscilla was not here. Mama and the casket were too much for her to handle; she surely didn't need additional reminders of what had happened so long ago, and what still caused her many nightmares. I could well remember her wringing her hands while relating just a bit of the incident to me. It pained her so much to speak of it; and hearing others talk of it so boldly would probably have been too much under any circumstances, to say nothing of the present ones.

A deep masculine voice broke in. An older gentleman whom I didn't know was changing the subject and making references to my mother's long and fruitful life, her fine character, and, again, how he had remembered her as a young woman: so very lovely, gentle, always delicate and fragile in appearance, yet strong-willed and determined. A woman standing near him, wearing a full-length mink coat — perhaps his wife — I thought I heard her say that she was Mama's cousin — was also remembering.

"Eva wore such beautiful clothes; she had such a flair for fashion. Why, I don't believe she ever wore the same outfit twice. At least they used to accuse her of not wanting to. And I remember those wide-brimmed picture hats she wore — looked so good with her tall, trim figure.

"And her hair — such a beautiful, deep-dark auburn — she could wear it in any style and still look good. She had the smoothest, whitest neck I ever saw — and the tiniest waist. 'Little in the waist; beautiful in the face,' they used to say of her." She looked around at my mother's still figure, then shook her head. "Has it really been that long ago?"

I thought I knew what she and the others were speaking about. I remembered seeing those remarkable, early photographs of Mama in the album; and I remembered the ones on the wall at home.

I was also remembering that invariably, to me, Mama had seemed to look older than she should. By most standards of that time, she was "old" when I was born — "much too old," many had been heard to say. "But when she was young, there were very few indeed — if any — who could 'hold a candle to her' — in looks, in style, in grace, in . . ."

Others in the crowd were disregarding their remembrances of Mama as a young woman and were, instead, speaking to the present — and how she had become reclusive in recent years — "almost from the time that Joe passed away, though for a while there she did go to church right much, and started dressing up again — believe that was the last time I saw her — at a church service at Bethany — or was it at Reedy Branch — to hear Sonny play the organ — must have been twenty years ago or more. . . ."

"Why, I would hardly have recognized Eva," a woman said [during the visitation] . . . remember how breathtakingly beautiful [she used to be]?"

"Little in the waist, beautiful in the face," they used to say of her.

(Eva Cornelia McLawton in 1913 at age 18)

Someone joined in: "Don't know what happened after Joe died — she just seemed to draw into a shell or something — when she began feeling so alone, I guess. She had stuck by him to the end — he had been so sick — after that, she started staying home more and more. If you wanted to see Eva, you had to go to her house — she seldom if ever left the house, let alone visited anybody — was just content to be at home, I think." The woman doing the speaking picked at one of the flowers on a crescent-shaped arrangement, then bent to pick up a fallen rose petal.

"I did hear that Rebecca Ann could get her to go for rides in the car sometimes during late afternoons, before she got sick." A man nearby nodded.

Mama, as she appeared in 1975, at age 80, when she had resumed attending occasional social events, and shortly before she became a confirmed recluse.

"There's no doubt about it, though, Eva had great influence, and was much loved. She will certainly be missed." At that, the woman raised her finger as though she had made a point of truth.

"Know it must really be bad on Sonny — heard that he didn't get here in time to see her before she —"

The woman making this remark stopped short when she caught my eye. She seemed uncomfortable with what she had just said.

Someone passing the coffin mentioned the casket spray and its companion piece, and others were commenting upon and admiring other floral arrangements, pointing out specific flowers and remembering how much "Eva loved vases of fresh flowers — just like her mother did — and she'd work for hours in her flower garden; and she'd share the nicest blooms with friends and neighbors."

The woman had introduced herself to me as "Cudd'n Milicent," in her obvious, but cultured, Southern manner of speaking. She was one of my mother's first cousins, on Mama's father's side.

Someone else added, "Why, I can remember when Joe would cultivate that garden for her just like it was a money crop. And people would come to see Joe and Eva in the spring and summer just to see Eva's flowers. Think Joe liked them as much as she did." The woman looked toward me and smiled.

I, too, could remember when I had been a child, how both Mama and Daddy would work in her flowers when there wasn't field work to be done. At the old home place, there used to be a fence around that garden, and I could remember lifting myself up by my hands just high enough to look over the wall; and I would see my mother and father hoeing or fertilizing, or planting. All the while they would be talking and smiling.

And I could remember Mama coming to the house, carrying a whole armful — or basket — of blooms she'd picked; and she would put them in every vase in the house — roses, camellias, dahlias, zinnias, hyacinths, tulips — in season — and snapdragons, gladiolus, irises, marigolds, larkspurs, jonquils — or, cape jasmines, sweet betsies — and some whose names I didn't know. It was certainly fitting that Mama should have flowers now.

And the azaleas, the dogwood trees, the wisterias, the magnolia trees: how I remembered the eagerness with which Mama watched them, in particular, bloom. She would have one of the workers — especially Tucker Allen — break several of the most beautiful of the magnolia blossoms with their waxy, green leaves from the lower limbs and bring them to her; and she would place them in every available vase throughout the house during summer, when they were in season.

Then, when fall and winter came, she would have Tucker cut the red-seeded cones from the magnolia trees, and again she would decorate the house with the beauty of nature; color and greenery, including pine, cedar, and holly.

* * * * * *

The same age as Rebecca Ann, Tucker Allen had been reared from childhood by Daddy, and our father had treated him like one of his own children. Daddy had given Tucker's widowed mother, Sophie, a light-skinned quadroon with Caucasian-looking hair (whom many had turned away), one of the tenant houses in which to live.

He gave her work in the house, where she assisted Mama with cooking and cleaning. She did Mama's washing, helped with the children, tended to the vegetable and flower gardens — anything that needed to be done.

Daddy taught young Tucker to farm: to hitch up the mules and plow; to plant, gather corn, prime tobacco, pitch hay, among many other chores; to do carpentry work, to be useful and self-sufficient.

Daddy even disciplined him (with Sophie's blessing) when the boy needed such. Both Sophie and Tucker loved "Miss Eva and Mr. Joe" more than they knew how to express in words.

Years later, when Sophie died, Daddy saw that she had a proper funeral, paying all expenses himself, and had her buried in the "colored cemetery," as it was then called, in a choice spot, under a sycamore tree — with an acceptable monument that he himself, with Tucker's approval, had selected.

Tucker continued to live in the tenant house, married, and with his wife had children there: a son and a daughter. Tucker Allen had helped Daddy from the time he and Rebecca Ann were ten years of age, continuing even after I was born and until I was seventeen — when Daddy died — and Tucker was 37 — and many years afterward.

I well remember how, on hearing that Daddy had died, Tucker had come to the house, asking for Mama, had stood by the porch to express his sympathy to her, and had cried without even a hint of shame. Mama, though grieving herself, motioned for him to come onto the porch; but "knowing his place," as his mother had taught him, Tucker remained where he stood — some distance away, in the yard, under one of the magnolia trees.

I remember that Mama — kind Mama (not caring about "status," "one's place," or "position") as it regarded Tucker — descended the brick steps, walked to where he stood, wrapped her arms around the grieving black man, thanked him, and spoke assuringly: "It's all right, Tucker. Cry if you want to; I know how much you loved Joe; he loved you, too."

Tucker — big, strong Tucker — fell to his knees at Mama's feet, held her hands. Mama called for some other workers in the yard to take him home, to see to his needs. Before he left with the others, Tucker swallowed several times to find his voice.

"Miss Eva, ma'am, do y'want me t' cut some flowahs fo' yo' — I mean, fo' Mr. Joe? I know h'much he loved yo' beautaful flowahs." Mama shook her head, smiled her appreciation. "Wait until tomorrow, Tucker. We have plenty right now; but Joe would be so pleased to have you say that — and to remember."

She wiped away some tears of her own as she turned, walked back up the steps, onto the porch, through the door, then into the hallway, and into her room. No one but Mama would have displayed such understanding during a time when she herself had need of consolation. She had gotten out of bed, where she so distraughtly lay, when she was told that Tucker had need of her. That was Mama.

* * * * * *

How Mama had loved beauty — anything, everything beautiful: the fragile asparagus fern; even the wildflowers that others viewed as mere weeds: goldenrods, honeysuckles; even the fields of small, pink and white clover; dandelions; straw flowers — all.

And again I was remembering — hardly a week had passed during her illness — and even before — when my aunts had not sent or brought her some flowers. Mentally, I was thanking them. I had thanked them personally before. I must do it again.

I looked over at the large design near the head of the casket — the arrangement my aunts had presented, the one

that Nathan had described as beautiful. I knew my mother would have thought so, too, and again I could hear her stretch out the syllable. "They are *beau*-tiful."

Someone was reading my mind. "Aren't the flowers lovely, Sonny?" The voice was familiar.

As I turned my head, the very pleasant face of Mrs. Evers, one of my former teachers, came into view. She hugged me and held my hand as she spoke in a distinct and articulate manner.

"I'm here because of you boys. You remember, I taught all three of you; and I have special memories of each of you. Certainly, I can empathize with your loss." She turned to look toward Mama, then back toward me with a sympathetic eye.

Mrs. Evers had taught eighth-grade English and spelling. She had liked us all, but Joseph had been her favorite and had also given her the most headaches. She remembered that with a smile and then became serious. "Son, the parking lot is full of cars — and overflowing. And just look at this crowd! Your family has a lot of friends; but, of course, that has always been obvious." She squeezed my hand again and excused herself, as she went to speak to Joseph.

I turned around to look at the casket. I was looking through people, familiar and unfamiliar faces. All were moving in slow motion it seemed, and pleasant murmuring pervaded the area.

I felt a tap on the back of my head. Robert wanted to know if I was all right. He had noticed my pensive expression. "Sonny — I said, 'Are you all right?'" He spoke more loudly so I wouldn't mistake the question. But how could I? He had asked that same question so often lately, kind brother that he was.

"Yes, I'm fine," I answered. He looked directly into my eyes for a moment with his hazel-green ones — to determine whether I was telling the truth — and then made his way across the room to speak to an associate.

A funeral home employee was handing me a buff-colored notecard. "A thin, older gentleman asked me to give this to you, Sonny — said he would not be staying."

I thanked the young woman, opened the note, and recognized the neat penmanship, in black ink, of Dr. Warren Johansen, one of my major professors of English at my alma mater, who, after his retirement, had worked with me as a copy editor.

In artistic, Spencerian script, Dr. Johansen had written a short but heartfelt message: "I am so sorry for your loss, especially because I know how devoted you were to your mother. Agnes joins me in expressing our sincere sympathy. W.B. Johansen."

Tears filled my eyes. Nathan held my arm, took the card from me, placed it in the side pocket of his blue jacket. "I'll hold on to this for you, Daddy." I nodded.

Questions came from over my shoulder, from beside me, and from in front of me. Nathan attempted whenever possible to answer all for me except the most personal inquiries. He was looking after his father as best he could, striving to make me comfortable and to keep me relaxed. He knew that much talking tired me, and tomorrow would bring an even greater burden.

Chapter 18

*E*VEN DURING SUCH A SAD AFFAIR as a funeral, even during a formal viewing, where respects are paid, a certain amount of small talk is often in evidence, easing the tenseness of the situation. Such was the case here, and now. Some of the men were discussing crops and equipment. Some professionally minded persons were discussing the progress of the medical school at the nearby university.

Some younger women were talking about their children and school, and other older ones discussed recent surgeries. Some relatives lined up age-wise, and began to reminisce. They were remembering school and college and weddings and trips. Someone hugged me and mentioned Mama's shroud and how becoming that particular color was. "Did you select that, Sonny?" I shook my head and explained that arrangements had been made by my brothers and sisters.

Some insensitive individual, some businessman whose face I didn't see, spoke about finances. "I bet Eva left a pretty

large estate — all of those tobacco widows were usually left well-fixed, you know — and Eva had considerable property of her own — know she never spent a lot on herself, though I've heard she gave a *whole lot* to the children." That was true — she had given a lot to us. But I never needed any material reward from my mother to know that she loved me. She showed that every day of my life for as long as I could remember. And she did the same for all of us, in different ways, at different times.

And the man was right. My mother didn't spend a lot on herself, but that was the way she wanted it. And that was her business. The man probably didn't mean to be unkind. I was taking matters too seriously again; I was overreacting. I must try to think of something else.

A few more hugs and smiles; and someone, noting my obvious sadness, made a lighthearted remark to lift my spirits. They meant well; they always meant well. A diversion of attention, and they were off. I had hardly taken a step back before someone was speaking to me again.

"Judge John W. Howard" approached and introduced himself, took me by the hand, told me that he was Mama's cousin, and that the woman on his right arm, wearing a silver-blue fox jacket, was his wife, Elsie — and Mama's cousin also — on the other side of the family. I could not make the connection, nor was I required to do so. They both spoke cordially; she kissed me on the cheek; he patted me on the back.

"Cudd'n Elsie's" accent sounded very dramatic, almost affected, though friendly; I later learned that she taught drama at the nearby university. As she was leaving to go to the other side of the room, she spoke over her shoulder: "It was my father who did all that research on the family tree in the early 1900s, Sonny. I've heard that you have painted some of the coats of arms. I hope to see them sometime."

Details again; details.

Then a quartet of persons pulled me aside, and all four — including the men — hugged me warmly, explaining their relationship to my mother. The red-haired man in a pin-striped, blue suit was a state representative: Mama's first cousin on her father's side; his late mother had been Mama's aunt. He fingered an ornate diamond-and-gold pocket watch and its matching chain and fob, telling me that it had belonged to my great-grandfather, his mother's father. He also carried a gold-handled cane, just for effect, it seemed.

Obviously proud of his importance, he was nonetheless immensely cordial and polite. His wife, a petite blonde, was dressed in black. On her shoulder she wore an enormous but gracefully configured, feather-shaped diamond broach, superbly crafted and styled: one of a kind, I was certain. *Why did I notice such things?* She smiled, but said nothing except to convey the usual courtesies — smiled again, and explained that "Aaron talks enough for both of us." I could not help but agree, though I did not comment.

"You remember Carlton, don't you, Sonny?" The man was speaking of his son. "He's your age, you know; he's now a criminal lawyer." I nodded my approval — that was congratulations enough. *All of my cousins enjoyed much success and affluence; and I was pleased for them . . . remembering . . .*

The other couple, both musicians, they explained, were related to both my mother and father; she a former opera singer; he a composer and orchestra leader. I had heard of them frequently — and of their accomplishments — and knew them both, but not very well. I had not seen them in years. The woman, "Cudd'n Mildred," much younger than Mama, made a point of citing Mama's proficiency at the piano and violin, as she had often heard her play when she had been a young girl. She and her husband, Eric, were two of the ones who referred to me as "Joe and Eva's baby boy." A word more, and they were off to visit with others.

Someone touched my arm and told me that they missed seeing me around town. I tried to smile my thanks. I was becoming sad; thinking of myself again, and why I was here tonight.

All the while, people were passing the casket, saying a word about my mother, remembering when they had last seen her, and deciding which of the children more closely resembled her. "Why, Sonny, *you* look like your mother. Never thought about that until now — and you look a lot like your Aunt Margaret, too. Believe you and Joseph and Priscilla look more like Eva than the others. The other children favor your daddy, I think." The remarks came from an older cousin. When I could not remember her name, she understood.

"It's been a long time, Sonny; but I have an excuse — I'm getting old, and I don't get out much anymore." She laughed softly, touched my arm, and was off with her husband to see another relative she hadn't seen in months, perhaps years.

The gathering here, for all its varied meaning, was much like a family reunion. These occasions were the only times that many were able to visit. No dishonor was intended if serious conversations gave way to lightheartedness; for these people had come to share happiness as well as grief, together with love and friendship. This way, they could visit many at once, though the main purpose was to see us and our mother, and to pay deserved respect to her life and memory.

But some, because of their upbringing or natural inclinations, sat silently in chairs and on sofas, almost in reverent observation, disinclined to talk in the presence of the deceased. These felt that sympathy was not necessarily symbolized in words, nor in deeds. Just "being there" was expression enough. And these persons would watch the time closely.

Several, on seeing the nine o'clock hour approaching, rose from their seats, eased their way across the room to where I was sitting, and said their unobtrusive good-byes. They left quietly, one by one, or in small groups.

Then, as though directed by an unseen hand, the whole crowd began to disperse. The conversational orchestra slowed in tempo and volume, until only a few utterances were heard; and these faded suddenly. Now, only the most familiar voices broke through the refrain, and presently there was an interlude of quietness.

I found myself in front of the coffin, and saw my hand on the shoulder of my mother. As before, I stroked the soft fabric of the peach shroud, and startled my own consciousness with one deep sob.

I was aware of nothing else except the form of my mother lying before me, cold and lifeless and unable to say the words I wanted to hear, unable to reach out and respond to me — to let me know that she forgave me for whatever it was I felt guilty of. I was a little boy again.

At once there were people at my side: Rebecca Ann, Francine, Robert, and Nathan. Joseph leaned against the wall nearby; his friend Dorcas was sitting alone in a chair, again aware that she must keep her distance. Rebecca Ann and Francine embraced me, even as I struggled against them. I was controlling myself as well as I could; my mother would not want unnecessary exhibitions; and I did not mean to be staging one. I was helpless.

The emotion I felt was overwhelming; every sense I possessed was on full alert, and I could not stop shaking. The flowers smelled too sweet; the silence was deafening; the breath mint was too strong; I felt a painful tingling in my face and hands. I was seeing too clearly, and not at all.

I was blind for a moment, but I felt Robert's arm around me, pulling me away, not forcibly, but imploringly. He guided me to the couch where he sat and held on to me with an arm around my back.

"I'm sorry," I told him.

"Go ahead, Sonny. Get it out. It's all right." He understood. After several minutes, he suggested that we leave. Other close relatives and funeral home personnel looked toward me, wanting to say something, but not knowing what or how.

Robert walked with me out the door toward the waiting car. His oldest son, William, would take me back "home" — to Mama's — where various family members and friends would be waiting to serve refreshments. Nathan and Bob followed. The others would be coming soon.

A numbness overtook me as William closed the door of the car and walked around to the driver's side. He pulled out of the parking space without a word, and slowed down as his headlights revealed the figure of Francine walking toward us. William lowered the window, and Francine handed me my glasses. I had left them at the coffin.

"Sleep softly, Mama," I heard myself whisper. William turned to look at me, but said nothing.

Chapter 19

MONDAY, DECEMBER 9, 1985, 1:15 p.m. The day seemed pale and bare, like so many leafless trees. The sun tried to shine but finally gave up and retreated behind the mass of heavy clouds. Today was the day.

In the sitting room, Dee was picking up a discarded paper cup and a napkin, intent on tidying up even when it didn't really matter. She wanted everything in place, and she'd see that it was, or at least try. She was dressed in navy blue, wearing a matching hat tilted to one side — well turned out and "fit to go anywhere," as my mother might have said.

I looked at her, remembering how often she had spoken kindly to my mother, how she had even been able to cause Mama to laugh at times, bringing out that subtle sense of humor that had been a part of my mother's personality. Dee had certainly become more than a nurse and housekeeper; she had established for herself a permanent place in the family — for now.

* * * * * *

Revelations not yet available would present themselves later, and when certain circumstances and questionable events became disclosed, they would matter a lot to some in the family — and not at all to others. We had little choice but to believe that Dee was as good and caring when alone with Mama, as when in the presence of Mama's children and other relatives and friends — although word would later reach us that indicated the contrary. Whether true or not, the major aspect of that "cloud of discontent" would never be reconciled to complete satisfaction.

For now — and for all time — nothing could be done to undo, to change, to alter the course that had been set by our mother herself. *She* had chosen not to be hospitalized; *she* had chosen not to have the prescribed surgery. So, she had to have help; and Dee had seemed the best choice of many candidates. Surely she performed her duties regarding Mama's care as well as she could — in the manner instructed by the doctors.

I had personally observed only one or two occasions when Dee might have been more alert to Mama's needs; but I could not interfere; I was home for just a while at the time and would be returning to my job in Texas. I could only hope that the others in the family were observing, keeping proverbial tabs on the situation, seeing that no neglect was evident — and that correct procedures were implemented when required, when desired.

After all, registered nurses were generally available — and in attendance — when asked to come and assist Dee and Rebecca Ann with Mama. Both Dr. Mallison and Dr. Jackson came whenever they were called. What if Aunt Margaret did find Dee asleep in the chair on an occasion or two; what if Priscilla and Francine did find Dee to be away from the house for more than an hour on three occasions, when she was supposed to be tending to Mama? Certainly there had to be reasonable explanations.

I had to lay aside anything that might upset me further. So, I tried and hoped for the best.

* * * * * *

Despite some questions that later arose as to her ability, training, diligence — even her consistent kindness or lack thereof — I would never forget Dee — nor would anyone else who cared about our mother. Yesterday morning, she had said to me: "Sonny, I just don't feel right. I got up this mo' nin' an' realized that Miss Eva wouldn't be needin' me anymoah, an' it was moah'n I could take."

I could see a big tear in her eye, but she gave a white smile and continued, "but, as I tol' yo' befoah, we have t' give it all up to th' hands of th' Lawd."

I really believed that Dee was sincere. I also had to believe that, regardless of how some others might view her, Dee, in expressing herself to me, had revealed her true nature, the exact way she felt. She had indeed given "it all up to th' hands of th' Lawd," while doing all that was humanly possible for Mama. For me to think otherwise at this moment would have killed me.

Now it appeared that Dee was rendering the last of her service in honor of Mama, and even in love for her and her memory. It was impossible not to view Mama with great affection, and Dee had appeared to find it easy to do. Even as she continued to busy herself with housekeeping

details, she showed how she cared. She stopped for a moment and looked at Mama's portrait above the mantel.

"In th' hands of th' Lawd, Miss Eva." She nodded as if to confirm her own statement. "I know Miss Eva was ready t' go — no doubt about it." She then walked to the other side of the room, stopping now and then to pick up a piece of paper or some lint off the rug, or to move a table or chair back into position.

Jill, my former wife, was helping her with some trays and was speaking softly to her. They were conversing about Mama, but I could not make out the words. It was only recently that Jill had begun visiting Mama again with regularity; and during those visits, she and Dee had become friends, able to discuss many concerns that affected us all. Jill had probably confided to Dee some personal details about herself and me, but that was all right. Illness of a loved one often brings out feelings of the heart and soul; and some feel compelled to share.

Jill was a sharing person, and a very caring one. It was natural for her to attach herself to someone who could understand and empathize. She had hugged me warmly this morning, reminding me of how it had been years ago; but there was no going back . . . *Jill had left such a scar upon my heart. I had given her so much of my life — "so fair a portion of my soul, my all"; of my everything. There was no way, at the time, that she could have perceived the utter destruction I felt. I would not let her . . . it was all too complicated, too inextricably bound, too . . .*

One of the trays crashed to the floor, and Jill looked in my direction to see if the sound had startled me. She knew my moods and thoughts.

I was sitting beside the piano, unconsciously running my fingers across the keys. Many were the times when I would sit in front of this instrument, admiring the gleam of its polished cherry wood that had delighted Mama. And, at her request, I would play some of her favorite hymns, and always the old standard "Carolina Moon."

"Play some for me, Sonny," she would urge. And always I did just that. As it is with all mothers, Mama probably thought I played better than anyone else she'd ever heard. To her way of thinking, there was something very special about her "baby" playing music for her. It didn't matter that I was not proficient. My keyboard skills were different from my mother's, and my touch not so refined, but she loved the sound of my playing nonetheless. She always smiled her approval. That had been more than enough reward.

Next to her family, music had been the most important thing in my mother's life. In later years, when she had become more and more accustomed to staying at home — and especially until her recent illness that had rendered her bedfast — she had occupied herself for many hours with her own music: after supper every night, for at least an hour; and on Saturday and Sunday afternoons; or whenever a free moment presented itself.

Mama and music seemed synonymous. Music and Mama were part of a picture, a pattern, much like the Three Graces that composed her cameo: Charm, Splendor, Joy.

She had entertained us all: our father until he died, my sisters and brothers and me, the grandchildren, great-grandchildren; her father and mother, decades before; her sisters, cousins, nieces and nephews; neighbors. We — and they — had all enjoyed my mother's music; her confidence at the keyboard; her sensitivity of expression; her refinement; her gentle character; the sum total of what she was, had been, and the memory she now left. *She was gone, but . . .*

Now, in the far corners of the house — the several bedrooms, the dining room, the kitchen, the screened-and-windowed-in porch — all through the house, even upstairs, were muted echoes: the voices of grandchildren and great-grandchildren — the way Mama would have liked it. *They* were music.

Momentarily, they were forgetting what today meant; that was the child in them. They would miss her more later, after all had been said and done, and when they would come to see her and not find her here.

Many of the younger ones didn't understand where she was, or why there were so many people everywhere at once, or why people were crying, or why there was an over-abundance of food in the house, or why they were constantly being told to keep their voices down. Some innocently asked: "Where's Grandma Eva? Has she gone off? Why is she not in her bed?"

Explanations from adult lips sufficed little, if any; for to these children, "Grandma Eva" was permanent, ever-present. To think of her as not coming back was beyond them.

Again — alone in my thoughts — I was unconsciously playing a melody that Mama liked, as I leaned toward the keyboard: a simple, haunting melody with my right hand, evoking from my mind the words I'd heard Mama speak, words of a song she had learned from her Aunt Mary — set to the tune of "Let the Lower Lights Be Burning" by P.P. Bliss.

Those words, by an anonymous poet, spelled out a philosophy appropriate for any generation. They held special meaning for me:

> Should you feel inclined to censure
>   faults you may in others view,
> Ask your own heart, ere you venture,
>   if you have not failings, too.
> Let not friendly vows be broken,
>   rather strive a friend to gain;
> Many words in anger spoken
>   find their passage home again.
>
> Do not, then, in idle pleasure,
>   trifle with a brother's fame;
> Guard it as a valued treasure,
>   sacred as your own good name.
> Do not form opinions blindly,
>   hastiness to trouble tends;
> Those of whom we thought unkindly
>   oft become our warmest friends.

"Should you feel inclined to censure faults you may in others view, ask your own heart ere you venture if [it] has not failings, too." I suppose that is one reason my mother never openly criticized another person.

"They are more to be pitied than censured," she had often said regarding wayward souls. "We cannot know what they might have gone through that brought them to this place in life. Before we judge — if indeed we ought — we need to try to understand, and help." My mother had lived her philosophy up until the very end. Assessing my own character, I realized that I lacked the ability to put her finer principles into action, though I had tried. But, that was all my mother ever required — that one try; the attempt was more important than the result.

Eva Cornelia McLawton as she appeared in 1915 at age 20.

Eva McLawton Ellis, photographed in 1972 at age 77.

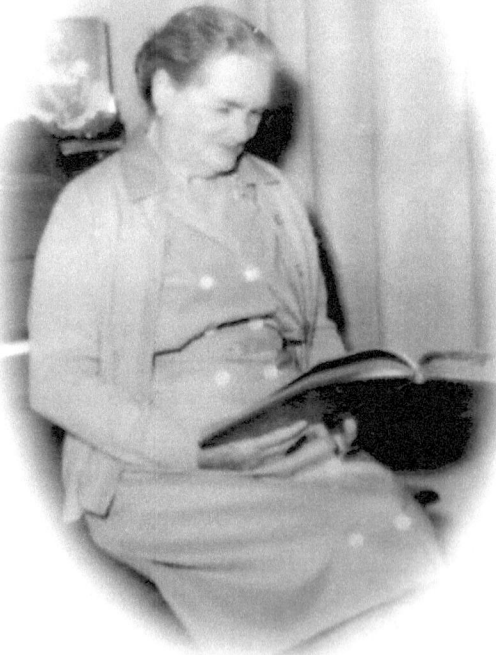

Literature, music, and all things beautiful had enriched Mama. "Should you feel inclined to censure faults you may in others view, ask your own heart ere you venture if [it] has not failings, too." Thus, Mama never criticized a person openly. "They are more to be pitied than censured," she had often said, regarding wayward souls. "Before we judge — if indeed we ought — we need to try to understand, and help."

She had taught us all that no one should expect always to win; failures were sometimes the greatest lessons. Still, one should not accept failure as inevitable. I almost smiled to think that my mother had truly been a philosopher, yet had not ascribed to herself anything more than motherly wisdom.

And that, she most surely had learned from her own mother, a possessor of many gifts of knowledge who could scold and love with the same vigor, but could make one feel secure in any circumstance.

My meditation was being interrupted. I felt Jill's green eyes on me as she motioned to our son to take me something to drink. Jill looked almost as attractive as thirteen years ago, but more mature. Her blonde hair made a nice contrast to her black suit — her still-fine figure — and my mental appraisal seemed almost fitting.

She had often asked me to help select her clothes, but had as frequently become frustrated with my indecisiveness. I was too difficult to please. I knew that now; I had known it then.

Still, it seemed natural that she should be with Nathan and me during a time like this. Divorce does not always kill friendship; I was glad that ours had survived. It was important to Nathan that Jill and I be friends; it had been important to my mother, too; and we all knew that. Mama would certainly be approving now.

Jill had heard me clear my throat many times during the past hour; and handing Nathan some cough drops, she insisted that I take one. I thanked her with my eyes as Nathan brought some soft drink in a cup, and the box of throat lozenges. I saw her catch a tear in a Kleenex; she then swallowed,

and smiled back at me, in an effort to cover the emotion she was feeling. *My beautiful Jill.*

Jill had always loved my mother as her own, and Mama had returned that love a thousandfold. I knew that Jill was remembering how often my mother had complimented her for being "like a daughter" to her. She had praised Jill's composure, her poise, her good looks. And Mama had allowed Jill and me our privacy; she had never meddled in our affairs, even during that terrible time of thirteen years ago when we had chosen separate paths. She had trusted that the paths, someday, would meet again.

Our paths *had* met again, but not quite the way Mama had hoped.

Chapter 20

THERE WAS COMMOTION ON THE PORCH, and one of the dogs was barking.

It must be Cleo, I was thinking, for Brandy still would not come to the house. Beautiful, white, loving Brandy, who had so often lay at Mama's feet on the porch, remained in the barn — sad, despairing, listless; would hardly eat or drink: missing Mama so.

Cleo, the old, black-and-white bird dog, could be equally as loving to Mama; but she did not express the same sensitivity, the same devotion to her mistress as did Brandy. While Mama lay bedridden this whole year, Brandy had sat or had lain at his place by Mama's chair every evening, waiting for her to come take her seat in the green rocker, until finally, after the stars had come out and Mama was nowhere to be seen, he would go back to wherever he had been.

He would return again and again; and family members (especially Robert and Joseph) would pet him, talk

to him, console him, even take him inside to see Mama. Making him leave was torture. He would cry; he wanted to stay with Mama, lie beside her bed.

Rebecca Ann, feeling so sorry for the poor dog, would allow him to stay inside for long periods of time, though she often had to walk around him to perform tasks — to do whatever it was she needed to do. She would speak to him for Mama, as Mama grew weaker. When Mama had been strong enough, she would talk to him herself; and Brandy would respond in a whimper — sometimes a bark and a thump of his tail — wanting her to get out of bed, to go to the porch with him. When she did not, he would drop his head to the floor between his paws and whimper softly. He could not understand what was wrong, or perhaps he could. . . .

Commotion on the porch again. The funeral director's assistant, Alfred, stepped through the doorway and into the hall. Speaking to Robert, he asked quietly: "Is everyone ready? We're lining up the cars for the procession — pallbearers in the first car after mine, then the family members — children and spouses according to age, then grandchildren and great-grandchildren."

I stood up and walked toward the hall; Nathan, Jill, and Dee close behind. I took my place beside Joseph and Robert, as Rebecca Ann and Francine stood across from us against the opposite wall. The several mirrors caught our images and threw them back at us — strangely, and in slow motion: reflections en masse that were captured in this wrinkle of fate, never again to be experienced this way: a picture never again to be seen.

Never again would the six of us — Mama's six children — be together. Time would tell; time would alter; time

would do whatever time wanted to do — without our help, and without consulting us.

Francine was picking at one of her nails, a habit that surfaced whenever she was worried or troubled about something. Nathan stayed close to his mother and Dee, occasionally touching his mother's arm to offer support.

Rebecca Ann's husband, Roland, was at her side, holding her trembling hands. This house was so full of Mama; and Rebecca Ann, perhaps more than any of us, knew the emptiness that now would fill it. She had frequented every room, every corner, every space — at odd hours — morning and night: checking here and there, securing the house, and testing locks two or three times, doing for Mama what Mama formerly had done for herself.

A sudden realization seemed to have stricken Rebecca Ann. Until now, she had been so busy doing for others that the fact of Mama's passing had not really sunk in. Her swollen eyes said a lot; she was not accustomed to much crying. She was strong. But last night and today had already brought a flood.

Robert was speaking to me. "You want to ride with us, Sonny — or with Nathan?" Then, with a glance toward Jill: "Since Jill is here, maybe the three of you could ride together, and Dee with you — whatever makes you comfortable." Then to Nathan: "You can drive for your daddy, can't you?"

Nathan agreed. "Daddy shouldn't drive."

Although we were not following protocol, Nathan, his mother, Dee, and I would follow the car that Robert drove. The important thing was to get to the funeral home and give our mother the proper memorial service she deserved. Formalities and adherence to established rules were fine and desirable, unless such caused discomfort for anyone — and our mother would never want anyone uncomfortable. Robert was much like her in that regard and would violate any rule — in this case, the "order of procession" — for the sake of making anyone feel better.

"Where is Priscilla?" Francine was asking.

My niece Hope replied that she was not here, just as Alfred, the funeral director's assistant, was pointing to his watch and telling Robert that it was time for us to be leaving. "What shall we do about Priscilla? We can't wait much longer." Alfred seemed a little nervous that one of the principals was not in place.

"I think we might as well forget her for the moment." Robert explained the circumstances surrounding Priscilla, how her being so distraught might prevent her from even attending the funeral. We would have to see to her later. She may, he said, be waiting at the funeral home, though that was unlikely.

The idea of funerals and their entourages bothered Priscilla. Death was more than enough; an organized procession emphasizing the fact that someone had died — especially someone dear — was out of the question. She could not be a part of it. We would have to allow her that privacy, even if such privacy did seem to dissociate her from the family unit.

"We'll have to leave without her," Robert stressed again.

We gathered on the porch, and paused momentarily. The cars looked too dark, even though highly polished. They seemed to form one continuous black line against the gray of the day — a black line broken only by the open doors waiting for us to enter.

Off the porch, inside the cars, and we moved in slow, slow motion toward the funeral home.

Chapter 21

JAMES MERRITT, ALFRED, and two more of his assistants traced a careful path through the random movement of the crowd inside the vestibule. We had entered single-file through the back door of the funeral home. We would have a few private minutes with my mother's open casket before the service — a last look at the tangible remains of her earthly body.

As we approached the closed double doors, the crowd moved away like an ebbing tide to allow us access. I felt a mixture of relief and pain, each sensation vying with the other for preeminence. Robert and Nathan were again at my side, and Jill behind me with Dee. The others followed.

We were swept into the viewing room where Mama was waiting. All floral tributes except the casket sprays had been removed and had been placed in the chapel. The many arrangements had been deliberately positioned on either side of a vacant space in front of the pulpit, where the closed

casket would complete the picture. We heard the hollow sound of the closing doors as they isolated us this last time, for these remaining few minutes of privacy.

The family members inside the room seemed to press each other too closely: children, grandchildren, and great-grandchildren, among other close relatives and spouses. Each of us would have one last moment with Mama.

Rebecca Ann was fingering Mama's hair in place, while fighting back the emotion that tried to come forth. Francine looked on with folded hands almost too tightly clasped. And again Joseph was holding up the wall.

Robert, in his usual manner, was trying to make everyone else feel better, his outward composure disguising his inner sadness. His expression was characteristically pleasant, though a strain was becoming apparent. He rested his left hand on the back of his head and pushed his black, wavy hair out of place.

He gripped the back of his neck to squeeze away the stressful pain. His hazel-green eyes held dammed-up puddles that tried to spill over. He picked at his right eyebrow and bit his bottom lip.

A unified feeling of sorrow pervaded this chamber, as was the natural course of things; and I found myself once more touching Mama and looking at her face, again experiencing the deepest emotion a child can possess for his mother.

But this time, I was to become the comforter. A grandson was reduced to sobs, as he acknowledged that he hadn't visited "Grandmama" as often as he should have. Then a granddaughter, and a great-granddaughter, then Jill, and Nathan, Bob, and Dee began to weep, each unleashing whatever it was they had kept bound up inside. I forgot my own loss and went to each of them to offer my consolation. The whole room cried; I was the exception.

For the first time — I didn't know why I hadn't realized this fact before — I suddenly knew that others felt as deeply as I, but had not demonstrated that feeling until now, or at least had not opened themselves in my presence. They had been conserving their energies and strengths for me, correctly appraising my needs — this must have been the reason. *I had encountered and met my sorrows; indeed, I had become acquainted with them.*

Perhaps, as always, my selfish concern for my own loss had prevented me from seeing outside myself. So deep was my pain that it had cut through my soul, but I did not own a monopoly on grief. I was not alone — and never had I been, except in those bleak moments of personal despair when I had separated myself from the others — because they "did not feel so deeply as I." Any barriers I thought to exist had been erected by me — out of fear, selfish regard, or misunderstanding. Dare I examine myself so closely?

Death had broken the barriers. At this moment, we were all in accord; we all loved Mama, though in varying degrees. And any petty differences we may have nursed faded now into forgetfulness. *Above all, foster understanding, appreciation, agreement.*

The ugly head of jealousy, or some other entity, intangible or otherwise, might later seek an encore. But for now, we could not allow such an intrusion. Yes, I was thinking: *At this moment we are in accord.* And though this awareness may have served to remind us of possible disputes —

real or imagined — we would not give entrance to them. Not now! They would have to enter later — on their own. Perhaps they would; perhaps they would not.

Months, possibly years, would pass before we would know. We would simply deal with those matters if and whenever they arose. Our mother had been a unifying bond and the arbiter of our rare disagreements. Her calm approach had stayed the few quarrels we'd had before they could become serious.

But now, she was . . .

One of the doors was opening. I heard voices outside; then someone was approaching me, and I felt a hand on my arm. A former associate had asked to see me; she had waited for a long while yesterday but had not been able to offer her condolences. I had been otherwise occupied.

James had let "Miss Verla," as I called her, in for this moment. He knew I would want to see her, and understood why yesterday had not been a good time. My flawless, brilliant Miss Verla held my hand, looked at me with unique understanding, then hugged me. We had talked about my mother on numerous occasions. She knew about and appreciated my devotion. She had a daughter my age. Now no words were necessary. She departed as quickly as she had come.

James Merritt closed the door and stood inside. He spoke to Robert, and we were being led to the family room. The funeral was about to begin. It was 2:20 p.m.

Chapter 22

ORGAN MUSIC BLENDED with hushed whispers as we found our seats in the family room. The two ministers were in place, sitting in large chairs with their legs crossed at the knee, and each wearing a dark blue suit. They both had visited us during various times in preparation for today, and they would now say whatever words they had planned, or whatever might be precipitated by their personal remembrances of our mother, or of us.

Their ministerial presence was obvious; a quiet, serene atmosphere prevailed, even as an occasional cough or whisper arose from the crowd.

The flower-draped casket was rolled in and came to rest on the carpeted floor in a position parallel to the pews. It completed that earlier picture my mind had drawn — it filled that vacant spot in front of the pulpit, and stood on the deep-red carpet, among the flowers. The casket, except for what my unwilling eyes had actually witnessed, could

be empty. Reality was running away; I wanted this to be a dream.

I wanted to wake up; I wanted it to be last Tuesday — I wanted Wednesday and Thursday and Friday and Saturday and Sunday, and most of all, *today*, not to have happened. I wanted my mother to be back in her home, even if confined to her bed.

"Just let me . . ." I pushed the words away. I couldn't stand to hear them even in my mind. I was breaking apart again. I must not.

I was thankful for the interruption. The officiating minister, the Rev. Nigel Latrick — the pastor of my mother's church — stood, signaling the congregation of friends and relatives to their feet. At his side was a valued friend, the pastor of the church in which I held membership: where I had attended for many years prior to moving out of state, where I had played the organ for nearly twenty years — had sung solos, had taught Sunday school, had filled the pulpit as lay speaker, had . . .

My momentary reverie had thrown me off balance. My sense of time was out of sequence. The congregation had stood as the casket was being rolled into place; but my concentration had been misdirected. I was seeing these as separate occurrences, rather than a simultaneous happening. I was tired; I was sick; I was not thinking clearly. Only one thing was certain, and I was making a futile attempt to deny even that. But the casket told the story, however hard I tried not to listen, or to see.

Nathan touched my arm to draw me back to reality. He had felt me shiver at his side; he had seen the color leave my face. He knew what I was feeling. His mother reached across his lap to hold my hand. I swallowed the persistent lump that was lodged in my throat.

I looked about myself to gather my resources, my strength, my acceptance of what was happening — of what had already happened. I enumerated my relatives in the family room. All my brothers and sisters, with the exception of Priscilla, were accounted for, as were their spouses. Eight of my mother's oldest grandsons were serving as pallbearers and were seated apart from us, in the main area of the sanctuary — close to the casket — and in the left front pew.

Other grandchildren and great-grandchildren sat in reserved pews to the right of them. The family room, where I sat with the others, was situated off from the sanctuary, but was equipped with a slatted viewing wall allowing us to see and hear, but affording us the seclusion we needed or desired. I felt glad for this isolation.

Glad? Maybe thankful, but certainly not glad. . . .

One of the kindest persons I had ever known was seated at the organ. "Corabeth," we called her; she had been our friend for as long as I could remember. She was rendering music in her superb style, with the exquisite expression that distinguished her musicianship and her style of playing. I heard the strains of Alice Hawthorne's "Whispering Hope," one of my mother's favorite hymns — a hymn I'd often heard Mama play on the piano at home, and one which she herself had sung in her operatic soprano voice.

The message of that song was so appropriate, so reassuring — if indeed I could countenance "reassurance":

Soft as the voice of an angel,
    breathing a lesson unheard;

Hope with a gentle persuasion,
    whispers its comforting word;
Wait till the darkness is over,
    wait till the tempest is done;
Hope for the sunshine tomorrow,
    after the shower is gone;
Whispering hope: O how welcome thy voice;
    Making my heart, in its sorrow rejoice.

But how could my heart, in its sorrow, rejoice — even with the gentle persuasion of hope that awaited Mama, awaited us, awaited everyone? I could not appropriate the hope that Mama had so often advised. Irony — supreme irony. "Hope will guide you through the night, till the early morning light," Mama had told me. "It is your greatest help — *never give up hope!*" I was supposed to be an intelligent man, but my mind and heart could not cooperate in this inward discussion . . . perhaps later. *If only I could draw a sip of hope from that brimming well.*

Corabeth had asked me last night what songs I'd like her to play for Mama. I mentioned several, and she had prepared her program with those, and had added others she knew to be suitable. Corabeth had also rendered music for our father's memorial service. The soloist, a minister friend, had also provided music for our father.

Mama would have been pleased. I knew that she would approve. Her service would be much like "Joe's," and nothing could have brought her more happiness during this final hour — if only she could know. I felt that she somehow did know.

Someone moved in to take the empty seat beside me; it had been reserved for Priscilla. Marvin touched my hand, raked his fingers through his curly hair, then whispered to me: "Priscilla is outside in the car; Tina is with her. Priscilla just cannot make herself come inside. I tried — Lord knows, I *tried*."

I nodded. I knew his difficulty. Their youngest child, a grown daughter, waited with Priscilla and would comfort her as best she could. Their oldest son was one of the pallbearers. He had tried to persuade his mother to join the others of us in the family room, but with no success.

Priscilla would grieve in her own way, and in her own isolation. I could envision her as she sat in the front seat of the brown car: shoulders straight, but with her head bowed and eyes closed. She would remain in an attitude of prayer and would be thinking of Mama with great intensity. She would be hurting beyond measure, not knowing how to ease the pain.

The organ pealed forth with the introduction to a solo. Beautifully rendered by a clear tenor voice, the old hymn sounded familiar, yet unfamiliar; it seemed endless — only because of where I was, why I was here. At once I wanted the service to be over, yet last forever. I understood, yet didn't understand. I felt helpless again. I shivered — again and again I shivered — and once more Nathan was touching my arm; his mother was holding my hand. The organ stopped.

A few moments later the minister was speaking. He described Mama as she had been as a young woman: her virtues, her life with her family, with Daddy, with us, and with the grandchildren and great-grandchildren. Her favorite Scriptures were being read: the Twenty-Third Psalm, and others.

The assisting minister, the Rev. Macon Tilson, was eulogizing Mama with words I had written, pausing to say to

everyone present: "I wish Sonny himself were able to read these words, but I know he cannot; so I will read them for him." Then, afterwards, and in his own words, Macon spoke to the present: how he had frequently visited my mother during the last year, how he had grown to love her smile, her quiet way, her special character, her dignity: everything about her.

For several minutes the ministers went on — first one and then the other — finishing appropriately with some words attesting to Mama's Christian example, her magnanimous deeds.

Macon Tilson read some fitting words from Proverbs 31:

> ". . . strength and honour are her cloth-
> ing; and she shall rejoice in time to come.
> She openeth her mouth with wisdom;
> and in her tongue is the law of kindness:
> She looketh well to the ways of her
> household, and eateth not the bread of
> idleness. Her children arise up, and call
> her blessed; her husband also, and he
> praiseth her. Many daughters have done
> virtuously, but thou excellest them all.
> Favour is deceitful, and beauty is vain;
> but a woman that feareth the Lord, she
> shall be praised. . . ."

A poignant pause from the minister's voice; and he concluded: "Miss Eva was uniquely special, as loving and kind a woman as ever there lived. As Sonny so aptly has said of his mother: '*She always looked beyond the unkindness of the world, and chose to search for whatever goodness there was to be found — and she never failed to find some goodness, somewhere — and in everyone.'* In this, and in so many other ways, Miss Eva did everything well; she lived her life to help others, though she never sought notice, recognition.

"At any time in later life — before she became so ill — she could have taken trips to foreign lands; she could have bought for herself anything she might have chosen, desired, or wanted: jewels and clothes — even more houses and lands. But she coveted nothing. Miss Eva was never one to guard her treasure. She desired little, except to love her family and others, to assist those in need — and this she did well, very well, exceedingly well.

"She would be embarrassed to hear the words I now say, for she was modest, unassuming — always approachable, available, yet pleased to remain tenderly reserved, quiet, and tranquil.

"She worked with her hands, with her heart, with her soul. Only Heaven will reveal how much good she did, how much she loved God, how many lives she touched . . . ."

Another pause, as obvious emotion rose into his throat: "I know I speak for all of you . . . within the sound of my voice . . . who knew her well: Her own works will 'praise her in the gates.'" He looked toward the family room, as though directly at me. Then he returned to his seat.

The last solo was being sung, the organ crescendoed in a final tribute, "Down the Road," and I could again hear Mama say that she was "going" her "last mile." She had known what she was talking about. I hadn't wanted to know.

The casket was rolled out with too much noise. I wished they'd stop. Nathan touched my arm. We were all standing. I followed the casket with my eyes until it rounded the corner of the sanctuary, being followed by the pallbearers.

Nathan tugged at my sleeve. "Come on, Daddy — come on." I reluctantly followed.

Chapter 23

SOMEONE WAS LEADING US out the back entrance
to the waiting cars. On the far side of the yard, under a clump
of loblolly pines, I saw a weeping Tucker Allen and dozens
of other workers who helped on the several farms. Standing as a group, the men held their hats or caps in their hands;
the women (some with small children) stood beside or between the men, with their heads bowed — all in honor of
"Miss Eva."

At various times, many of these had come to the back
door at Mama's home to offer condolences, to express their
personal sorrow. They truly loved her, and had to make it
known.

Their presence here was unusual — a departure from
that which was considered proper in this society, during
this era; but how *glad* I was to see them, to know that they
cared enough — even against tradition — to gather this
way. I wanted to go to them, to thank them, but I was being

led and guided by funeral home personnel; I was being prodded toward the waiting car. I could not break away without causing some disruption in the proceedings. I resisted the inner urge to comfort Tucker Allen, especially — as I had seen Mama do when Daddy had died. *Tucker Allen, whose loving heart was so full and overflowing, as before . . .*

Except for Mama's kind acceptance of them in life, this band of workers might never have felt comfortable enough to present themselves to her — to us — in this setting. But what a beautiful tribute, what a remarkable expression of caring they showed! Never for a moment had Mama acted as if she were below or above anyone. *Mama had made everyone feel at ease, even when she had suffered immeasurably . . . even now when she was gone.*

A hum of voices, soft plaintive cries — as if music from a hurting soul — rose from the "imposing crowd" (as some in Mama's family might view them): the familiar tune of a poignant spiritual and its stirring words: "I look'd ovah Jordun, and whut did I see, comin' fo't'carrah m' home? A band of ainguls, a'comin' aftah me; comin' fo't'carrah m' home. Swing low, sweet chariot, comin' fo't'carrah m' home; swing low, sweet chariot, . . ."

My heart joined those kind souls in song, until Jill, with a gentle touch on my shoulder, jolted me back to the "business" at hand. She whispered: "Get in, Sonny." She motioned toward the front seat of Nathan's car. "Get in." There were tears in her eyes.

We had been led out of the family room all too quickly, with unnecessary haste. Now we were ushered to the waiting vehicles — for another processional. We were in the cars, but now we were waiting. The long, black hearse was out of view, but in my mind I could see my mother being rolled toward its gaping door. They were putting her in place. And in front was the police car with its flashing lights. The flower-filled van was positioned directly behind the hearse, and the family cars were moving into a tighter line. Minutes became proverbial hours as we waited for the procession to begin moving toward the cemetery.

Nathan placed a firm hand on my arm as I strapped the safety belt around my waist. I was not always so diligent; I could not understand my need of the safety belt at this point — we would be driving slowly — too slowly, yet too quickly.

Jill and Dee both had hands on my shoulder and were leaning forward in the back seat. Dee reminded me again: "Give it all up to th' hands of th' Lawd, Sonny." This time, her voice was a command rather than a request. I swallowed without speaking, and Jill increased the pressure on my shoulder to encourage me toward the resignation I needed.

"*Whispering Hope.*" Again the words of the song roared in my head: "*Making my heart, in its sorrow, rejoice.*" I absolutely could not rejoice, did not want to rejoice. . . . *Hope? An ideal, yes; but could my future exceed the promise of the past of which that song spoke so eloquently? I wondered,"when the dark midnight is over," could I, with assurance, "watch for the breaking of day"?*

Down the street, a few turns, through an avenue of evergreens, and we were entering the gates of Bayden Cemetery. Uniformed officers stood on either side.

Around and around we circled, mausoleums and simple gravestones, a blend of rich and poor, old and new, the

elderly and the young, and those in-between. The yellow canopy punctuated the spot. All but too cheerful in color, it stretched above the grave of my father and the freshly dug one into which my mother would be lowered. The shelter it offered was uninviting, yet compelling.

Rows of chairs had been placed beneath the canopy, at the side of the grave; and they seemed to mock me with obvious emptiness. Though covered with a warm brown fabric, they appeared cold — colder than the weather.

The flowers were being put in place around the grave, and people were getting out of their cars and advancing toward the area. I opened the car door to get some air. A slim figure in black, a niece I had not seen, eased by and touched my hand without speaking, knelt beside me for a brief minute, and was on her way to stand at the site. More car doors were opening and closing, echoing against the tombs and trees, and disturbing the mute air.

One of the funeral assistants was directing us to the chairs, as Mama's coffin was borne by the tender hands and strong arms of her grandsons. The casket slid into place, and someone guided me to the far end, at the head of the coffin.

Nathan and Jill and Dee sat next to me, the others beside and behind. I couldn't see. I couldn't even feel at this moment. Many people were standing around, but I was still alone: at a great distance, far off, in a world devoid of persons and things. In a day or two, I would be flying back to Texas. Again and again I expected to hear: "When are you coming home?" The question now would come from my guilty conscience.

Both ministers made formal statements, said more kind words that floated above and outward, then prayed individual prayers. The words "ashes to ashes, dust to dust" reverberated inside my head; and presently both ministers were extending their hands to me and other family members.

People began moving away into familiar pattern-like units, family members together with close friends. Later, many of these would gather at Mama's to render post-burial consolation. That was their way.

I was left alone in my chair. Nathan touched my hand. I could feel my head shaking as I quietly chastened: "Go on. Let me alone for a moment."

I stared at the blue-gray thing in front of me, knowing that it held the only remains of my mother. And I was wishing her back, yet coveting her release. Near the head of the casket, James had placed the simple floral tribute I had given: a satin heart with a single white orchid. It soon disappeared behind a wall of water.

After a long while, I arose from my seat. Unsteady legs carried me somewhere, but not far.

There was one more thing I must do.

Chapter 24

I STOOD SILENTLY ON THE GREEN CARPET at the foot of her grave. I became aware of a group of faceless friends and relatives waiting to speak to me, a blur of gray and black against the dull sky. I confronted them slowly, then turned for one last look toward my mother.

I reached out and barely touched the coffin, letting my finger slide gently over the cold metal.

"Good-bye, Mama," I whispered. Then I backed away.

"Please — just let me die," she had said.

Though it was not my intention, I suppose that's what I had done.

EPILOGUE

The characters in my story all have wonderful memories of my mother, though these memories are colored with grief and remembrances of her enormous suffering.

Naturally, some questions come to mind: How would we have done things differently — or were we right to remain resolute, steadfast in our promises? Did we act wisely in allowing her wishes, even against what may have been our better judgment at the time? Did we have any real choice in the matter, since our mother was adjudged competent by her doctors?

In the final analysis, was not her decision the one that really counted? Lest we are made to feel too guilty, we must believe that matters transpired just as she wanted them to happen. At least we allowed her the privilege (and right) to be at home where she wanted to be, and, most importantly, to die with the same dignity with which she had lived.

We miss her, of course; but we would not want her back against her will — and certainly not so helpless and so confined as she was those last several months. To be thoroughly objective regarding our mother is impossible, and we found it hard indeed to wish for her what she wished for herself. Yet, to do less would dishonor one who truly represented the *epitome* of honor and goodness.

All of her children and close relatives except me, perhaps, can believe that they did what they could to make her happy. She was such a kind and gentle person. "Sleep softly, Mama" seems the most appropriate benediction.

— Noel Thomas Manning

Afterword *2004*

• After he had finished reading my first draft in late 1986, my brother Robert asked me very pointedly, over the telephone: "Sonny, did you — have you been able to — do what you said you were going to do in your Prologue?"

"What do you mean?" I was puzzled by his question.

"Finally lay our mother *'to rest.'*"

I honestly could not answer him in the affirmative then — and, now, eighteen years later (after his inquiry), I still cannot answer the question with any measure of self-conviction. I do not know whether I will ever be able to forgive myself fully — *and lay her to rest*. After all, I was the "holdout." I was the only one of the six who refused to sign the papers of consent to have the feeding tube installed. I would not give even a verbal agreement when Robert and Aunt Margaret called. I alone declined to afford my mother weeks and possibly months of extended life.

I also resisted going "home" — returning for an extended stay to be with Mama and the family — when my mother insisted and fairly begged me to do so. *"When are you coming home?"* That question will forever haunt me.

One friend who saw and talked with me daily — in an effort, no doubt, to soften my overwhelming sense of responsibility — suggested that there was a higher purpose in my being away from the others. "Had you been there in Bayden with your brothers and sisters," she exhorted, "you may have been persuaded to 'cave in' and agree to the extraneous means your mother resisted and clearly did not want. You should certainly take comfort in knowing that at least you kept *your* promise."

For me to "take comfort," however, required more than acknowledging logical advice and reasoning. At the time, I could not extend intelligent rationale to include emotional tranquility. Even now, with the passage of years, I still cannot reconcile the dilemma.

My brother Robert, recognizing the perplexity I faced, the bewilderment that confounded me, and the indecision that tore me apart, tried so hard to help. He approached me the same way he had approached our mother — with an abundance of common sense.

Robert — kind Robert — assured me countless times, during conversations over the phone and in face-to-face discussions: "Mama would *never* be able to rest — or to be at peace — knowing that you blame yourself for something that is not *your* fault, something that cannot be *undone*. You know she would want you to be happy, not sad the way you so often are."

Early in 1980, just a few weeks before I left North Carolina to assume my new position in San Antonio, a romantic interest of mine gently advised that when my mother's death occurred it would doubtlessly affect me in the most dreadful way. (My mother was enjoying excellent health at the time.) Alicia had observed my affection for my mother and thought it excessive, an evaluation I thought odd since she demonstrated a similar attachment to her father.

But Alicia was right: My mother's demise did affect me terribly, but since the romance between Alicia and me had faded, she was not on hand to see just how badly I took Mama's death. But my brother Robert (who knew Alicia very well) was on hand. Because he was so observant and attentive during "that terrible time," Robert (perhaps more than the other siblings) did see and understand how very horribly I was affected by our mother's illness and death.

The handsomest of the Ellis boys, Robert was immensely charismatic; and when a young adult, he had "girls falling all over him," to use a popular expression of the era. His blue-green-yellow eyes were of such an unusual color and expression that they mesmerized many fair ladies during his prime; and, with his wavy black hair, perfect white teeth, ready smile, and trim physique, he never lacked for attention — though he had eyes for only one: the girl he married.

Robert would die of a sudden, massive heart attack in March of 1998 — at the age of 65 — having been pronounced "fit" by a team of doctors only days previous to the attack. On my rare trips back home to North Carolina, I still visit his widow and see some of his children and grandchildren. I have only good memories of Robert and am fond of all his family, as they are of me. His son Bob (mentioned frequently in the story), the youngest of the children, at 38, is the age of my son, Nathan; and still resides in Bayden with his wife and son.

•My brother Joseph, who had saved me from drowning when I was four, experienced a complete and utter change of personality after our mother's death — though astute observers may have noted inconsistencies already in evidence then (and even earlier), and a gradual worsening of certain problems.

Our Uncle Emile Clemmons, Aunt Lucia's husband, at her insistence, tested Joseph's IQ — "just for fun," when Joseph was a very young man. Not surprisingly, Joseph scored "high genius plus." A re-testing produced the same result.

Intelligence tests administered in grammar school by district educators had shown Joseph to be exceptional and immensely gifted. Similar testing in high school revealed even more impressive aptitude.

Teachers had always touted his brilliant mind, but Joseph was not fond of studying — did not like school, period. He much preferred to play pool at the local billiard parlor from which our father often ushered him back to class or to the principal's office.

Joseph, like all of my siblings, was much smarter — a lot more intelligent — than I, though I had performed well in school. Additionally, he, like the others, displayed a considerable amount of *common sense* — something sadly *lacking* in me.

As to work, Joseph liked the outdoors and was happy to work with his hands. He made his living as a farmer and landscaper. I personally thought it a sad waste for him not to use his remarkable genius toward advanced education. But upon reflection, I know that I had no right to prescribe any course of action for him — though I did presume to question some of his activities after the death of our mother.

During his last years, Joseph's behavior became "less restrained," to say the least. He would (in Southern vernacular) "throw away" a home, a business, two wives, several saddle horses (who were almost his life) — even personal respect and esteem. His last three years were immensely troubled and painful (both physically and emotionally). He turned to strong drink, abused himself terribly, and suffered a horrible death from liver disease and intestinal cancer in April of 1988, less than three years after our mother's passing. He was only 52.

It was often said of him: "When he was good, there was no one better; when he was bad, there was no one worse." I honestly never knew a man with a harder head or a softer heart.

At the time of his death, Joseph lived with our sister Francine, who still worked at a nearby manufacturing plant. He was found to have died alone at Francine's home by our oldest sister, Rebecca Ann, who came as usual to bring his mid-afternoon snack and to take him for a ride out in the country.

There were those among his acquaintances who thought that there was "more to Joseph's death than met the eye," as they expressed it. Toward the last, he had associated with some persons of questionable reputation — especially just before his demise. What their "business" entailed, no one ever knew — but Joseph had lost large sums of money gambling. It was told that a silver cigarette lighter, not belonging to anyone in the family, was found on the premises shortly after his death.

Some persons in the community were said to have observed a strange car in the driveway only hours before Rebecca Ann found him dead. A coroner's inquest did not bring to light anything other than "natural causes," although there were said to be some strange marks on Joseph's throat.

Despite Joseph's fall from public grace, his nieces and nephews remember him as a remarkably generous and considerate uncle.

I remember him as one of the most accommodating and caring brothers a person could ever hope to have — though I feared him when he was drinking and was not himself. Were it not for his being so alert — and quick to the

rescue — during the incident at the creek (when we were both young boys), I would not be alive to tell this story. For that, I shall forever be thankful.

•My youngest sister, Francine, would develop dangerously high blood pressure, acute diabetes with its sundry complications, and for four years would reside in a nursing facility because she required around-the-clock supervision and care. Just previous to the time of her hospitalization, she was found lying on the floor of her residence — unconscious — by my brother Robert who had gone on one of his regular visits. He, with the help of police officers, was forced to break into her home, as her adult sons were both out of state at the time and unavailable to provide entrance.

Francine died in November of 2000, shortly before her seventy-fifth birthday. As I was recovering from surgery at the time, I could not attend her memorial service, which was held in Bayden.

Like our father, Francine demonstrated an innate propensity for mathematics. I recall many occasions during family gatherings (before she became ill) when I would "test" her ability. I would say: "Frannie, add these for me, please — in your head." Then I would call out a long list of triple-digit numbers I had written on a piece of paper (the sum of which I had already figured). She always achieved the correct answer — and in short order — even when I would throw in some subtraction to break her concentration. Remarkable! Family members present always joyfully applauded her gift, and challenged me to show *my* skill. I invariably declined.

I also remember Francine's bright smile, her laughing eyes, her enchanting personality. I still see her in my mind as the beautiful, colorfully dressed young woman with gardenias in her black hair.

• Aunt Leela, the aunt closest in age to Mama, would die after a lingering illness less than three years after my mother — March 1988 — one month before Joseph. She would die of the illness that had begun developing when I saw her at my mother's funeral in December of 1985.

Although the cause of Aunt Leela's death was never officially diagnosed, most family members believe it resulted from an aggressive cancer of the stomach — although she was hospitalized for a short while with pneumonia. Again, because I was ill and had undergone serious surgery, I was unable to attend Aunt Leela's memorial service also held in eastern North Carolina. Kind, unassuming Aunt Leela was in life — and will remain in memory — the quiet aunt who exercised moderation in all that she did.

• Aunt Lucia, a mere week later — March 24, 1988 — would be found by Aunt Margaret, with whom she shared a large home, to have died from an apparent heart attack, suffered during the night. For a whole week prior to her death, Aunt Lucia had lain ill with a flu-like virus — but appeared to be recovering. Regretfully — and again, because of health problems — I was unable to attend her memorial service.

Aunt Lucia, the brilliant, sophisticated, sociable aunt who had met with congressmen, ambassadors, and diplomats, and who had conferred with important persons in many fields of endeavor, expressed graciousness in confidence. In a position of authority, she tempered every command with remarkable charm. She was much admired and envied for her ability to negotiate compromise against enormous odds. She had no

difficulty putting one "in his place," but made the offending person feel comfortable there.

•Aunt Margaret, who had been so insistent upon the extraneous means of life prolongation that my mother resisted — in particular the feeding tube that "might bring Eva out of this and keep her from starving, and at least help her feel better" — would fail very noticeably during the mid- to late-1990s. She would deteriorate slowly in mind and spirit — even physically — until it was deemed necessary to admit her to nursing facilities where she resided for almost a decade.

For a few years, after becoming ill, Aunt Margaret was able to recognize and interact with family members. On some of my trips back home, when visiting her in the nursing facility, I would note that she derived much joy and contentment in my playing the piano for her (and for those assembled) and leading them in singing old favorites. She was hardly ever in my presence, when a piano or organ was available, that she did not ask me to play — which I gladly did, as I had for my mother.

Early on, in her illness, Aunt Margaret was diagnosed with Alzheimer's disease; she would suffer with advanced dementia compounded by brain damage resulting from accidental choking while eating, and would lie unconscious for several minutes before being found by healthcare personnel. After being released from the hospital, she was understandably transferred to a different nursing facility.

I last saw Aunt Margaret in late 2000. Although carefully confined (sometimes restrained for her own safety), and ill to the degree that she was unable to converse well, she did appear to recognize me. For a long while, during that last visit,

she clung to my shirt, appearing to want me to stay (as I was leaving); and she told me that she loved me — a sentiment she very seldom expressed to anyone, ever. The nurses on duty that night told me that they had not observed her to be that alert and interactive in a long while. She tried very hard to tell me something, but could not communicate verbally whatever it was she wanted to say. I can only trust that she knew that I was "Sonny," in whom she had once set great store.

Aunt Margaret would die in the Bayden area in February 2002. Because of illness, I (again) would be unable to attend her memorial service. Considered a teacher of the first order, an educator who set high goals for her students and assisted them in accomplishing those expectations, Aunt Margaret is still remembered fondly and respectfully as one of the premier educators in the system — by university officials as well as the few fellow teachers still alive who remember her. I routinely see persons, on my return trips to North Carolina, who tell me that my Aunt Margaret had taught their grandparents, their parents, and themselves; and wish that she were around to teach their children. That is how highly she was regarded in her field.

Whether intentional or not, both Aunt Margaret and Aunt Lucia would teach a very hard lesson — something I will never understand. Any favor accorded me was somehow to be lost forever — but gradually — after 1985, as evidenced by a change of deeds and wills which deprived me of any material bequest at their deaths. I never asked them for anything, and I hasten here to say that I saw in writing — on one occasion only — what they promised me orally. But I never doubted their word, and, indeed, advised them that they "ought to divide it all among the several nephews and nieces, for there is enough to go around." Those who did inherit from their estates did so legally. Of that, I am certain.

Some explanation is no doubt in order, and I know that I may risk being misunderstood; but I feel compelled to speak this piece. While I cannot — and would not desire to — attest to any influence that may have been exerted upon them by other family members, I cannot help but believe that Aunt Margaret in particular was urged to channel in other directions what she had promised me: furnishings, valued photographs, the old Victorian home, et al — including the inheritance from Aunt Lucia (in Aunt Margaret's immediate control) that was to come to me.

Perhaps there was not an enormous amount remaining after the expense of years and years of care; I do not know; I have no way of knowing; I will never know — although before their deaths, both aunts told me that there was a considerable amount "to be had." They did not boast about such matters, so I can only surmise that they were absolutely forthcoming in what they said to me and in what they promised. But that is past.

Admittedly, the ones who may have benefitted from the estates did much for Aunt Lucia — and for Aunt Margaret, especially, during her declining years. They could not have been better to Aunt Margaret; I stress that fact; and I do not begrudge them their inheritance or anything they received from her, or from Aunt Lucia — but to deny me at least a portion of my promised inheritance reflects behavior not consistent with the rest of the family.

Everyone knew that I had been considered "special" to these aunts. If those who inherited erred in any manner

as regards what was promised to "the favorite nephew," they will answer to their own conscience. I wish that they might have, at least, answered my letter of inquiry. I heard — only recently — that Aunt Margaret's ancient Victorian home, a place where I had enjoyed staying many days and nights, has been sold. How I would have valued the ownership of that home — not only because of its historical significance, but also because of its nostalgic appeal to me.

I honestly hold no bitterness; I value my memories today, just as I esteemed and admired the aunts themselves when they were alive. After I began earning my own money (late in my teens and while a young university student — and continually until they died), I sent them cards, gifts, and flowers for every occasion, as they and I enjoyed a special bond. I took them places; I ran errands for them; we visited older family members together — some of whom I had never met and who had inquired after me, and who knew me as "Eva's baby."

Almost without exception, on such visits, older relatives whom I did not know would remember me as "the little boy with blond curls and blue eyes, who always turned red in the face when anybody spoke to you." Upon observing me as an adult, they also would smile and comment, as though surprised: "Why, you even turn red *now*." (I still blush, after all these years.)

I began doing little deeds for my aunts well before they advised me of any bequest they had in mind for me; it did not occur to me that I would receive anything, for I was not thinking ahead, or of their passing.

Indeed, everything I did for them, I did from my heart with no expectation of repayment. What I did for them, I did

because I cared about them. I truly loved them; and I believe they loved me. That is really what matters.

Nevertheless, on my first trip back "home" in 1986 — a year after my mother's death — I learned that Aunt Lucia, in conversation with close family members, had been heard to reflect: "How could *Sonny* — of all people — have allowed *that* to happen to his mother?" I doubted that she had been understood correctly, since Aunt Lucia well knew how horribly I was affected by "the event." *How could she expect me to have acted differently?*

Yet, in a rare, unguarded moment that week (during one of my invariably pleasant visits with her and Aunt Margaret), she said directly: "Son, didn't you *understand* that you were *causing* — I mean — *allowing* your mother to *die*?" *Could this be another of those horrible nightmares that had plagued me so?* She repeated: "Did you not understand that you were causing your mother to *die*?"

Aunt Margaret, sitting beside her on the pink sofa, touched Aunt Lucia's arm as if to caution her. And, on seeing how deeply the thought (to say nothing of the question) had hurt me, Aunt Lucia quickly rose and walked across the room to embrace me, and added what (at the time) sounded like very empty reassurance: "I'm sorry, Son. I should not have said that. I *know* that you would never intentionally hurt or cause pain for anyone — especially not your *mother*."

She then patted me on the back in her characteristic manner, kissed me on the cheek, returned to the sofa, and changed the subject to more pleasant matters.

Even after the apology, my visit with them was ruined; and I had to leave immediately to contain the overwhelming emotion. Inside the car, I let go; and the pent-up tears broke

loose in renewed abundance. The rearview mirror caught reflections of Aunt Margaret and Aunt Lucia on the porch as they waved their subtle good-byes. Aunt Lucia was dabbing her cheeks with a Kleenex. I had to believe that she had not meant to be cruel, but was speaking out of her own frustration at having lost a dear sister she thought could have been saved. Enormously sensitive, Aunt Lucia sometimes made hasty remarks that she later regretted — and for which she would try to make amends.

It was also well-known in the family that Aunt Lucia had not approved of my marriage — not that she disliked Jill, but because she considered me not sufficiently gainfully employed at the time. In this instance, she soon capitulated with a gift of money and a beautiful, sentimental card wishing Jill and me a long and happy life together.

I do not lament being deprived of my portion of the material inheritance from my aunts so much as losing my standing in their high opinion (if indeed I did lose that). I intend here to explain how I have been made to feel — not knowing why, not knowing what may have caused them to change their minds in my regard.

Something did happen, and I honestly do not know what, or why, with any real assurance — though comments made to me, and some which "came through the grapevine," as the expression goes, should have put me on notice — especially as regards my mother's last year and how Aunt Margaret and Aunt Lucia viewed my decision to "let" Mama die. *"It would be kinder to take a gun,"* Aunt Margaret *had said.*

As trusting as I always have been, I chose to dismiss most of the unfavorable information that came my way.

I still do; and I neither desire nor expect recompense at this point; I merely speak to the matters between my aunts and me and the fond accord we always shared.

If I disappointed them to the degree that has been suggested, that is totally beyond my comprehension. How can one disappointment, one failure to please, destroy a *lifetime* of favor and goodwill? *Surely not after forty-five years of fond regard!*

I never, ever looked upon any of my mother's four sisters except with the greatest esteem and love. They knew that, and I knew that; and that truth I can take to my grave.

Material and monetary rewards are useful, yes; but memories and affection cannot be bought, erased, or taken away. They will always be mine (because I embrace them) — and I can live with them, and die with them. I may be lacking in many qualities, but sincerity is not one of them.

•My oldest sister, Rebecca Ann, at 85, still lives two miles east of Bayden in one of the old, ancestral family homes that dates from the Civil War period, and which tradition says was built (or at least completed) "by the women, since all the men were away fighting in the war." Inscriptions on one of two identical, symmetrical main chimneys denote dates from the 1860s to the 1890s; some inscriptions, though barely legible, indicate dates before even 1860, and several sets of initials. These markings, I am told, reference transfer of ownership, surveyings, repairs, et al.

As is often the order of things, the old home (referred to as "the manor" in some documentation) has fallen into disrepair, but it provides a great nostalgic comfort for me. As a child, I (along with cousins and other relatives of my

generation) frequently played under that old house. It sat high off the ground — on large, thick brick pillars — and when a young boy, I could stand up and walk around under the house with ease. Since that time, the yard has been filled in with at least three feet of soil and sod. The brick pillars are no longer visible; cement blocks and brick underpinnings hide those vestiges of the past. Indeed, the old house does not "hover over" those who now approach, as it once appeared to do.

Missing from the yard, where it held a very prominent place when I was a child and even as recently as ten years ago, is the ancient pomegranate bush. Age, disease, and the natural order of things have taken their toll; no longer is that coveted plant standing atop its mound of earth, where for a hundred years it had blossomed, borne fruit, and changed with the seasons.

The pomegranate bush became significant to me because it had belonged to my paternal grandmother whom I never knew — Daddy's "mammy." The bush was introduced to me when I was a little boy by my paternal grandfather, who viewed it in an almost reverent manner (in treasured memory of his "dear Adelaide," my father's mother).

In spring and summer, when I was a child, I often sat under the shade of that large bush, and when the blossoms would burst forth with their scarlet-orange color, I invariably would pull one and take it to Pa. He would caution me in gentle tones not to pick the blossoms: ". . . for the bush will not bear any fruit if all the flowers are pulled."

He would then pat me on the head and tell me that he understood why I had picked the flower for him, for he thought it was very pretty, too. "But, now, don't pull off any more of the flowers," he would chasten with a smile. "Let's wait until the pomegranates grow, and then we will pick some of those when they are ripe — and we will enjoy *them*."

I would wait for weeks and weeks, watch the flower petals twist and fall, the fruit form and grow larger, change from green to a reddish hue, until finally in October, when the fruit was about the size of an apple, it would be ready. Pa would pluck one of the red pomegranates from a lower branch. Then, with his sharp little pocketknife, he would cut open the big, orange-red ball and slice me a piece. He and I together would pick out the seedy fruit with our fingers, taste the tart, fresh taste of "Mammy Adelaide's pomegranate." I thought I was in Heaven. That family ritual continued between my grandfather and me for as long as Pa's health remained good.

After Pa died in 1947 — and well into my adulthood — every October, I would wait for the pomegranates to ripen and would feel a sense of contentment that cannot be described in mere words. Rebecca Ann, knowing the "story" and my fondness for pomegranates, would always save at least one for me — and would invariably pick the very first ripe one for her "baby brother." Mama had Tucker Allen to plant a pomegranate bush especially for me, when I was about twelve — a sprout from the ancient one at the old home place. Sadly, it died the same year that Mama did — a strange coincidence to be sure.

Today, here in San Antonio, I have a pomegranate bush planted in a very large pot in my backyard. With eagerness, the little boy in me still watches for its blossoms to form, then its fruit — but for some reason, my bush does not bear, though I care for it as best I can. *Perhaps some-*

day . . . "when the shadows flee away," to use the words from an old, old song.

Friends here in San Antonio who know me well are aware of my fondness for pomegranates. Every year, when I can find the fruit in the produce section of grocery stores, I buy two or three ripe pomegranates and dry them in the air and add to my collection. Dried pomegranates claim many prominent spots in curio cabinets in my home, on this table and that, on stands — just everywhere.

The last time I was back home in Bayden, I stood in the yard of the old home place with Rebecca Ann, and in the exact spot where Mammy Adelaide's pomegranate bush used to be (the southwest corner of the front yard). I felt a warmth of spirit and love — and longing — that less sentimental souls might view as foolish, but my sister understood why my eyes had "watered up." She had to look away momentarily, as she perceived what I felt and was empathizing too much.

In declining health, Rebecca Ann nevertheless still drives a car, enjoys the recreation of bingo, and dotes on "Sonny," whom she still refers to as "my baby brother" and whom she views "like one of my own children."

Rebecca Ann's husband, Roland, a retired Army officer, died suddenly in December 2000 of a heart attack. Her first husband (the father of her five children) was found to have died from a gunshot wound to the head in October of 1960 — in a vacant tenant house on one of the farms, in which dried tobacco was being stored. Many in the family (as well as many in the neighborhood) thought that he had been murdered by a close relative, but that was never proven. I was a witness after the fact, as I stood watch with Rebecca

Ann and her daughter, Hope, as law enforcement officials, investigators, and the county coroner scrutinized the area.

When allowed, I (nineteen at the time) entered the house with Rebecca Ann and saw the scene after her husband's body had just been taken away; it was a gory sight.

Among other, more gruesome, evidences of the death, I spotted on the floor a small fragment of her husband's skull bone (approximately three by four inches in size), which the coroner had failed to take away. I felt a strange compulsion to reach down and remove the bone fragment from Rebecca Ann's sight; I drew her attention away from it, but she asked if I thought it was part of "Albert's skull." I told her yes. I told her that I expected other county officials would come and remove additional remains, which they later did.

•My sister Priscilla, though quite ill, remains cheerful of voice and attitude, and at 82, is a recluse. She lives in a historic city about forty miles northwest of Bayden. She still suffers from Meniere's disease, is devout in faith and practice, and continues to contact me on a weekly basis by phone and letter. She refers to me as her "very special brother."

Acute in mind, spirit, and memory, she occupies herself with the writing of poetry and family history: times, events; and illustrates her own stories. Her husband, Marvin, died suddenly in late 1996 from a brain hemorrhage. Her daughter, Tina, still lives with her; she has two older sons, one of whom lives in Canada.

Regretfully, Priscilla has never recovered emotionally from the near rape she experienced when she was sixteen. Nightmares are a regular occurrence still. Priscilla, who has suffered perhaps more than any of us, nevertheless thinks

of others first. She calls, writes, phones, sends cards — always with cheer, understanding, and a cause for gratitude in all circumstances.

I have some very distinct remembrances of Priscilla when she was young and so attractive — in particular, the expert manner in which she arranged her auburn-chestnut colored hair in an immensely becoming pageboy style, with every strand in place — and her neatness of dress, her well-pressed appearance, her slim figure. (She favors Aunt Leela, as we say in the South when someone resembles another family member in physical appearance.)

Older members of the family tell of the long curls Priscilla wore when a teenager, which drew many compliments from classmates and from friends at church and other meetings where she and my other two sisters sang in trio. Once, she had been happy and well, outgoing, joyful, even though forever sensitive and easily hurt by cruel words.

One of her classmates — perhaps thinking he was being "cute" — once made an untoward remark to her regarding the near rape Priscilla had experienced — and only a week or two after the incident. Sadly, that remark still occurs in dreams that Priscilla has to this day. *Whether intended or not, unkind words can cut to the core.*

It is important for the reader to understand that Tucker Allen, the respected black tenant who loved my mother and father so, was *not* the "trusted worker" who broke into our home and attacked Priscilla. The reader may confuse Tucker with my sister's attacker because both their mothers had worked for my family; and both Tucker and Priscilla's assailant were about the same age and had also worked for my father on the farms.

Tucker (called "Peter Pan" by many in the community) continued to work for my family well into his seventies, and died suddenly in 2001 after a few years of declining health. Tucker was particularly fond of me (and I of him), and I sought him out whenever I could on my visits back home. He well remembered when I was born "that cold Tuesday in 1939," as he recalled.

In later years, when he felt comfortable to do so, Tucker fondly teased me that four-year-old Joseph, not especially happy to learn that Mama had a new baby, had threatened to "sleep under the house." It seems that Joseph could not bear to have anyone usurp his position as the favored child in the family.

•Jill, Nathan's mother, has remarried and resides in northwest Florida. She and I maintain cordial contact through the shared interests of our son and his family. She is still immensely attractive, personable, talented. Her lyric soprano singing voice remains one of her chief attributes.

•My niece Hope, still fetching at age 63, operates a business of her own, and is, as well, a teacher of line dancing — a current trend in many locales. She and her husband live on a large farm they own four miles east of Bayden. They have a son who is the age of my son, Nathan; and two older daughters.

•My last contact with Dee was the day of my mother's funeral. For some time, my aunts, my brothers, and Rebecca Ann did see her occasionally.

I still think of her favorably despite some questions raised regarding her diligence. There were questions raised as well regarding her integrity. After Mama's death, some

items were found to be missing from the home: articles of clothing (dresses, sweaters), a pair of "Sunday" shoes, their matching bag, a few pieces of jewelry kept in a bedside drawer, and some money that might have been taken by any number of persons who had ready access to the house.

Because she was the "stranger" on the premises, Dee was singled out, though never approached directly, to my knowledge. A few of my more vocal (now deceased) relatives nevertheless suggested that she was at least "careless," and at worst, "less than totally honest." I personally doubt that she was really *dishonest*.

On one occasion, while I had been sitting with Mama — shortly after Mama had been confined to bed, and during my visit to see her in late 1984 — I observed Dee in an adjoining room, as she examined and carefully stroked a black suede purse belonging to my mother. I was standing in the doorway, and Dee turned and looked at me with no hint of surprise, and said in a matter-of-fact voice: "Sonny, y'think yo' mothah might min' m'havin' this pocketbook? Looks like it hav'n been used in a while, an' it's s' pret'y."

"I'll ask Mama, Dee. I doubt if she will really *need* it anymore." When I approached Mama with the request, she replied in her usual gentle and generous manner: "It will be quite all right, I suppose —" and then, hurriedly — "Why, of course — let Dee have the purse." Then Mama whispered, as if to herself: "*They must think the end is very near.*" She had obviously heard the conversation between Dee and me from the adjoining room.

I could not understand Mama's intoned statement, for it was she, after all, who had set the events in motion by refusing the surgery. It must have seemed unkind, none-theless, to be distributing her personal effects in advance. I nodded my permission to Dee, and she redeposited the suede purse into its protecting cover, and then into her personal overnight bag. Mama's eyes caught mine for a moment; she nodded, smiled, and then turned her head. She whispered again — this time some private something to herself, which I felt disinclined to question. Maybe it was a prayer.

At that moment, I felt as if I had betrayed her — as if I again were abandoning the duty my father so long ago had decided for me: to take care of Mama. I motioned to Dee, as unobtrusively as I could, to return the purse to its rightful place. She read my expression, retrieved it from her bag, and said with a smile: "Y'know what? Maybe Miss Eva can git really dress'd up agin 'fore too long, an' can use this purse. Won't that be'a pret'y sight?"

I nodded, and turned with a smile in my mother's direction. But my mother, characteristically, kindly chastened: "I said that Dee could have the purse, Sonny, so give it to her." And then to Dee: "Now, put it back with your things. Enjoy it." But Dee shook her head. After that experience, I tried very hard to see that everything of Mama's was kept in place, thinking, perhaps, that by doing so, I was holding on to Mama for a longer time.

On one of my last trips home, however — during "that time," the fall of 1985 — and shortly before my mother's death, the suede bag, along with a pair of matching shoes, was found to be missing. And yes, later, other items among my mother's personal possessions were gone.

It is entirely possible that in conversations with my mother, Dee might again have admired certain items that

Mama thought — or by that time had decided — that she would no longer need. It is possible that Mama simply gave these articles to Dee without advising anyone in the family of the gifts. I prefer to believe that is what happened — if the missing articles wound up in Dee's possession. After all, as I stressed earlier, my mother often "gave" without consulting, without informing, without even thinking that she was doing anything out of the ordinary.

Certainly, though, if Mama could have known of the possible suspicions surrounding some of the missing items, and had she indeed made gifts of those to Dee, she would have been quick to set matters aright. My mother would never allow anyone's character to be questioned without cause, and even then she would be the first to defend and offer an explanation, if she knew of one.

I doubt if I shall ever see Dee again. Our paths never cross, and I have not been able to contact her. Even if I were to see her, I would never question her. I prefer to remember her kindnesses to Mama; I prefer to dismiss the doubts, the unsubstantiated accusations made by some in the family. "What is done is done," as it is often expressed in the South.

During the late 1984 visit with my mother (the time of the "purse" discussion), I noticed on Mama's right cheek an unusual, red area that extended to her upper lip: what appeared to my layman's eye to be a burn. When I questioned her, Mama reluctantly told me that someone had served her very hot coffee, and that she herself had spilled it accidentally.

A similar burn appeared on the right side of her neck. Rebecca Ann, knowing how the injury would affect me, tried to alert me beforehand so I would be prepared, then explained that our mother would not tell anyone how "it" had really happened, except to say that she had spilled the coffee on herself, which Rebecca Ann doubted. The doctors thereafter insisted that any beverage or food served to Mama be tested on one's wrist, as one would for an infant, to avoid another such incident.

A week and a half into the visit, I noted that the burns crusted over, then turned black, and peeled. (Ointments which the doctors prescribed were applied every few hours and hastened the healing, leaving no discernible scars.) To this day, no one has accepted responsibility, although one of Mama's sisters suggested that "someone tending to Eva must have been very careless." My mother, however, never complained. She asserted that "it is nothing to worry about," that the burns were an unfortunate accident — nothing more. That was Mama.

On one of my trips back home — shortly after my mother had been confined to bed (still able to eat a normal diet, though she was quickly deteriorating and suffering) — my brother Robert spoke to me referring to Dee. He and I were going to "Mama's" from the airport, where he had picked me up about a half hour earlier that night.

He spoke of Dee's herbal remedies and how devoutly she believed in their medicinal qualities; he asked what I thought regarding those "cures." I replied that I did not know what kind of remedies she might be suggesting, but I personally had no objection as long as they remained within the guidelines of our mother's doctors' prescribed care.

Then I added, no doubt unadvisedly: "If you don't watch it, Robert, she'll be feeding those herbal teas and soups to Mama in great abundance, and will keep her alive forever."

Certainly, I did not mean my assertion to sound the way it must have fallen on my brother's ears.

Robert very quickly, but kindly, retorted: "Keep her alive forever? Why not? You don't want Mama to die, do you?"

The words stabbed my heart, and I explained immediately: "Oh, no! I don't want Mama to die — but I don't want her to linger on in pain."

Robert cleared his throat: "Well, she's not suffering so much right at the moment. She does have a lot of pain, but for now it is not unbearable." He looked at me with a quizzical, rather horrified expression, then turned his eyes away from me.

At that precise moment, I felt a gulf fixed between my brother and me; but that would be bridged before the night was through. He knew that my insensitive-sounding words did not reflect my heart. Mama had already made me promise . . . when her time came.

•My cousin Clarice, the registered nurse (only child of my late Aunt Trillis), and I had been close over the years. Since my teen years especially, she had (as we say in the South) "made a lot of me," as did her mother. Clarice would travel twenty miles or more, without hesitation, to aid someone she knew to be in need, especially if her knowledge of medicine and health care could be of value to that person — night or day. On more than a few occasions — to my personal knowledge — she took persons — even strangers — to doctors "here, there, and everywhere." She was one who put care into action, not just in words.

One special "thing" that I shared with Clarice was her affection for India peacocks with their glistening plumage, their fan-spread tail feathers, lit by the sun. The male birds are especially beautiful while strutting, and "courting." Clarice and I both considered these fowl the most beautiful of God's creatures. I enjoyed so much the many times I visited her and her husband on their farm east of Bayden, when I would have the opportunity of walking in the yard with them under the pines, and have the peacocks come close to me, unafraid, in their richly colored, plumed regalia. What beauty — what glorious beauty!

I never will know what happened between us to cause Clarice's favor to lessen, if it did; and I sincerely regret losing with her something that was quite important to me. Clarice would die in March 2001 after a heroic battle with a recurrence of cancer. She was never one to lament or to speak of herself except in the most enthusiastic of attitudes.

If one inquired after her health, she would characteristically say (even to the end): "Oh, I'm fine." She contended that most people made such inquiries out of courtesy, without truly desiring to know how the person really felt at the moment. She was also fond of saying that to love others was a commandment, but that she did not necessarily feel obliged to *like* everybody. If anything, Clarice was plain-spoken.

•Drs. Mallison and Jackson and I remained friends for many years. Sadly, Dr. Jackson, to whom I felt really close, died suddenly during the early 1990s while vacationing in the Bahamas with his family. (One of his daughters is the age of my son, Nathan, and was in school with him.)

His father, the elder Dr. Jackson, whom I also knew very well, was the doctor who delivered both my brothers and me; and who had hoped that my mother might miscarry while carrying me. He later told me — when I reached my

Dr. Jackson and the author during one of our pleasant visits in Bayden. Friends for many years, Dr. Jackson and I shared mutual love for all the arts; he himself was a superb musician. I shall never forget how kind he was to my ailing mother.

early teens — (upon reflection, and in his caustic, yet affectionate manner): "Well, Sonny, my boy, you know you nearly killed her — but if you try hard enough, you might prove to have been worth all that trouble you caused your poor, poor mother — but that remains to be seen." That kind of remark was typical of Dr. Jackson the elder. What came from his mouth as an apparent insult was generally an indication that he liked the person. *Wonder if he still would like me, were he alive.*

On my every return trip "home," Dr. Jackson the younger would call me, or I would call him; and we would visit in his office, or have a meal somewhere, and enjoy time together — and even reminisce about his father and mother ("Dr. Brady" and "Miss Feliah"), whom I remembered and who had expressed fondness for me. The younger Dr. Jackson and I shared mutual interest in the arts — in particular: music, painting, writing, drama. Although he could appear gruff and unyielding like his father, Dr. Jackson demonstrated special affection for older persons (as did Dr. Mallison).

I personally witnessed Dr. Jackson's interest in my mother's well-being, as he had held her hand, knelt in front of her chair (while gently patting her badly swollen leg), and pled with her to have the broken hip repaired. I will never forget his kindness.

•I, "Sonny Ellis," the narrator of this story, still reside in San Antonio, Texas, where, for twenty-four years, I have served as managing editor and director of publications for a private foundation. I have been engaged in the Christian publishing industry from the time I was 18, and a freshman in college. *My father had hoped that I would eventually pursue a Ph.D., but that was not to be in the course of time, events, and circumstances unforeseen. But had he lived . . .*

At 64, I continue in my work as a church musician: organist, pianist, choir director, soloist; and lay speaker. I still paint in oil, write poetry, essays, short stories, and music; and am currently working on a major novel. Like my late father, I enjoy ballroom dancing immensely. While suffering from some ongoing health problems, I nevertheless maintain an active, productive life. I travel back to the town of my birth (Bayden) whenever possible — generally only once a year.

I admit wholeheartedly that I am a complex individual with a highly developed, sensitive nature. I do regret my bent thereto, for it has been correctly surmised that,

on occasion, one has to "handle" me with kid gloves. I do, nevertheless, care for the downtrodden and try at all times to find something good in those whom society deems the "worst" of individuals.

And, like my mother — but perhaps to excess, in my case — I love all things beautiful. But, I would not change that part of my personality for anything in the world. I have to remain true to myself — to borrow some advice from the literary genius of centuries ago.

Nathan as he appears today: 2004.

•My only child, Nathan, at 38, is an educator (as is his wife) — and is a radio and television personality, a videographer, and an award-winning documentarian. He holds a degree, with honors, in Communications/Drama. He did work-study in Russia as part of his undergraduate degree, and, interestingly, discovered some of his tapes, films, and documents missing upon returning home to the United States. He believes that he inadvertently photographed something classified or perhaps not pleasing to the powers that be, even during the time of *glasnost* and *perestroika*. Nathan presently serves as assistant director of public relations at a private university in western North Carolina, where he lives with his wife, a seven-year-old daughter, and a four-year-old son.

•Eva McLawton Ellis, "Mama," is buried in the family plot in Bayden Cemetery, beside her beloved husband, Joe. In the same plot, I will be buried (when my "time comes," to borrow my mother's phrase) in close proximity to my parents and to my brother Joseph, as I have never remarried. Everything remains in readiness for that eventuality: The monument stands in place already.

•Blond, blue-eyed Joe Ellis, "Daddy," my father, died in November of 1957 at the age of 65. He battled heart disease and numerous undiagnosed health problems for at least twenty-five years prior to his death. My first remembrance of him was when I, a very young child, was allowed to visit him in Duke University Hospital (Durham, North Carolina).

He lay gravely ill, was said to be suffering from inoperable stomach cancer, as well as heart disease and various other maladies of undetermined origin. He was not expected to survive, and since he had asked to see his "baby boy," the doctors allowed a child under twelve years of age to visit a patient, which was against all rules at the time.

Mrs. Mobley, my father's private nurse at Duke, conducted herself with strict professionalism. She was every inch a nurse, as the expression has it: with starched, white uniform; nurse's pin on her lapel; white fold-back cap with striped markings, white stockings and shoes. Stern, aloof, ever serious, she frightened "little Sonny," but Mama assured me that Mrs. Mobley was "helping Daddy get well."

Sadly, Daddy never did get well and was in and out of hospitals every year, weeks — even months — at a time, for as long as I knew him. Mama never left his side during those times. I remember specifically, when I was in the sixth grade, that Daddy remained in the hospital for three months after a heart attack, lay under an oxygen tent; and then, in 1957 (his last such stay), he again was hospitalized for three or four months, and never regained sufficient health to leave the house thereafter except to go for doctor's appointments, to which I often took him. As sensitive as I was (and am), watching my father suffer so during that time was understandably horrible for me — perhaps more dreadful than seeing him suffer thus when I was a young child.

An incident occurred during my father's hospital stay in 1957 that I will never, ever forget — and which grieved everyone involved to an enormous degree. This incident nevertheless gave me insight into the despair that my father's impending death was causing him.

SATURDAY AFTERNOON, 12:30 P.M.: MARCH 9, 1957. I stood beside my father's bed in his private room in Pryde Memorial Hospital located in Greenview, ten miles north of Bayden.

Unable to breathe well on his own, Daddy lay under an oxygen tent. He was slowly recovering from a massive coronary thrombosis — one of the most serious, the doctors had said, that they had ever seen that had not resulted in sudden death — and Daddy was especially vulnerable, because he had endured other heart attacks and suffered from advancing heart disease. This last attack had destroyed a large portion of his heart (in particular, major sections of the right ventricle and auricle), and his body was retaining fluid — something they had expected.

"The buildup will worsen," the doctors told family members. "Mr. Ellis is developing heart dropsy" (a term used at the time to describe his condition and type of edema), they

warned. They administered periodic injections of a mercuric oxide solution to help expel the fluid that was beginning to fill his lungs, his abdomen, his legs and feet.

But in recent days, Daddy had rallied; he seemed to be improving greatly, though the doctors had told my mother that this progress was only temporary. Even at best, he would be in the hospital for at least another four to five weeks, they had advised.

"And, do not get your hopes up too much," they cautioned, "but cheer him as best you can. Help him understand that his condition *is* improving — don't worry him with what might ensue in the weeks to come. For now, be grateful that he is doing better."

For two months — ever since the attack — my mother had stayed with him day and night in the hospital room, refusing to leave his side. Daddy had made it clear that, even with registered nurses available, he required my mother's loving support, her "company" — and *she* wanted to be with *him*, as well. Daddy was justifiably afraid — and my mother was immensely worried, though she tried to conceal her great concern.

Family members brought changes of clothes and whatever else Mama needed to the hospital, for she would not leave Daddy. Her vigil was constant, unyielding — the only time she left my father's side was for her own daily grooming, which she did in the private bathroom adjoining Daddy's room.

The hospital had kindly allowed a chaise longue to be brought in for my mother to use during the night (or whenever she desired), but she very seldom moved from the chair beside my father's bed: alert to his breathing, his call, his

every need. She herself was showing signs of increasing fatigue, but she refused to admit any discomfort or inconvenience — so devoted was she to my father.

Standing by his bed this Saturday afternoon, I had just given Daddy some cherry-flavored Jell-O and several sips of water — something Mama ordinarily would have done — but today she was not at her "station." Her four sisters (Leela, Trillis, Lucia, and Margaret) had come for her at 9:30 this morning.

"Eva needs to get away for a while," Aunt Margaret had asserted; and though my mother expressed great reluctance to leave, even my father urged her to go, saying that since his "baby boy" was here with him, he would be quite all right for a while.

"But please come back before night, Eva," he had requested. Mama assured him that she would be gone for "only a few hours." Gripping my left arm, with her right hand on my cheek, she looked at me intently, telling me with her eyes not to leave Daddy's side. I understood.

My sixty-four-year-old father and I had exchanged a few words of conversation while I served him the Jell-O and water; and, although very weak, he was nevertheless talking a lot better, if not in his usual strong voice. As always, I reiterated my encouragement, which at seventeen I no doubt did not express quite so well; but, I did the best I could, and he appeared to appreciate my being with him and the momentary respite from the nurses who hovered over him.

And while he wished that "Eva would hurry back," he well understood how "she might need a change of scenery," as he expressed it.

Along with my attempts at cheering him, including "I-know-you-will-be-better-soon" encouragement, I told him about my upcoming piano recital (which I knew that Daddy would not be able to attend). He asked the title of my "piece" — as he had not heard me practice — and I told him, "The Warsaw Concerto." Amazingly, he remarked that he knew something about the piece and thought that it had been written about the time I was born — 1939 — and by an Englishman named Richard Addinsell, for a "war film."

My father's familiarity with the piece surprised me, for, in actuality, I did not know that he had much knowledge about so-called sophisticated music, although he loved and often sang the old standards. There were many things that I did not know about my father. Time would reveal that I knew very little indeed.

Aware that I should not tire him, I cautioned him not to talk, to save his strength — but asked if he wanted some more water, or perhaps some juice. He shook his head, and I placed the water glass back on the metal cabinet beside his bed. I closed the flap of the oxygen tent, but left it unzipped so I could peep in on him, and speak to him if need be.

I took a seat beside his bed and listened to the hum of the machinery that pumped the oxygen, and heard the beeps and chimes outside the room, and overhead voices from the speaker system, as nurses and doctors were being called to assist other patients in rooms up and down the hall.

My father fell asleep, and slept soundly (and peacefully it appeared) for about two hours. I dozed off in the chair but soon awoke to the sound of soft voices behind me as the door opened. In walked Mama and her four sisters. I recognized the faint fragrance of Aunt Lucia's expensive perfume,

and I heard Aunt Leela speak in her gentle tone: "Why, how nice. Both Joe and Sonny are resting so well." I looked at my watch. It said 3:05 p.m. (I had heard the attending nurse, just outside the door, tell my aunts that they could "visit with Mr. Ellis for a while, but do not tax him any more than necessary — he needs to conserve his strength.")

Although I could not see her, I heard Mama assure the nurse that she would make certain that no one would "tire Joe unduly." Aunt Lucia and Aunt Trillis stepped past me, whispered, "Hello." Both had vases of flowers in their hands; Aunt Trillis's offering was one of her magnificent African violets. They quickly but quietly placed their flowers (among several other arrangements) on the long TV table beside the bathroom door, but well within my father's view.

Aunt Leela (who looked so much like Mama) nodded in my direction, smiled, and walked quietly to the opposite side of Daddy's bed, and stood there clutching her brown purse in front of her — and, characteristically, held a lace handkerchief. Aunt Lucia joined her.

Aunt Trillis, turning from the flowers, cordially snapped her very blue eyes at me, as usual (in fondness), and spoke just above a whisper: "How is your father feeling, Sonny?"

"Pretty good for the moment, I think, Aunt Trillis. Thank you."

Oddly, I thought, Mama had remained with Aunt Margaret just inside the door, but behind the folding screen that allowed privacy for Mama when she reclined on the chaise longue at night.

Why had she and Aunt Margaret not advanced with the other three?

The commotion, though not out of the ordinary, roused my father. Daddy turned his head from side to side, as he customarily did upon awaking, took a deep breath, and was presently fully alert. He swallowed a few times, and I asked if he might like some water. He shook his head.

From her vantage point, as she peered around the screen, Aunt Margaret observed that my father was now awake. She stepped forward; and in her usual, authoritative voice — and this time seeming quite pleased with herself — she spoke directly to my father: "Joe, we have brought a very pretty woman to see you."

With that, my other aunts extended their hands toward my mother, as Aunt Margaret ushered Mama to the side of the bed. Aunt Margaret motioned for me to pull back the flap so that Daddy could clearly see. Momentarily, I was unable to move. Aunt Margaret repeated: "The flap, Sonny — pull back the flap, so that your father can see this very pretty woman."

Mama, a very different-looking Mama from the one she had been when she left at 9:30 this morning, came into view. I saw her, but did not see her. The transformation was astonishing.

She looked ten years younger, and she was smiling. She looked prettier than she had in years. She wore an elegant sheath dress with a subtle pattern in various hues of blue and pink, with navy high-heeled shoes with gold caps on the heels and a matching navy bag trimmed in gold metal. She carried a lace handkerchief and wore navy blue gloves.

Around her neck, she wore a double strand of golden beads, one strand slightly longer than the other, which complimented the portrait neckline of her dress. On her

ears, she wore matching earrings. On her right wrist, she was wearing the ornate gold bracelet bearing her scripted monogram and decorated with engraved roses and ribbon swirls — the bracelet that Grandpa John had given her on her seventeenth birthday: a treasure from the past.

A henna rinse had been applied to her hair, enriching its natural auburn color; her hair was puffed and set in deep waves that caught the light, and was tied in a large French twist at the back, with a mother-of-pearl-and-gold ornament. Mama looked stunning — better than I, personally, had ever seen her. She was wearing heavier, but tastefully applied, makeup, with noticeable rouge and darker lipstick than usual — and even a hint of mascara on her lashes. Though already trim, her figure looked somewhat slimmer, no doubt owing to a new girdle and bra (I blushed at the thought) — and she carried herself with her usual erect posture; and this time, she looked regal.

But my father was not pleased. He looked hurt, despairing — almost angry, I thought.

Aunt Margaret, so eager to hear Daddy's compliment and approval, urged Mama closer to the bed. "Look, Joe — doesn't Eva look beautiful — I mean, *really* beautiful?"

Daddy said nothing, turned his head — then, back toward Mama. By now, Mama, in all her new finery, her fashionable upsweep, her totally attractive appearance, showed noticeable discomfort. The four sisters all chimed in their praise of their "prize" until Mama lifted her hand ever so slightly to quiet them.

I observed my father's hurt, along with that which my mother also obviously felt. Finally, my father spoke — words that no doubt pierced my mother to the core: "Eva,

couldn't you wait for me to die?" He repeated: "Couldn't you wait for me to *die*?" Standing beside my mother and realizing her pain and observing her wounded expression, I thought that *I* would die. Mama stood still, said nothing.

But Aunt Trillis was not quiet: "Oh, Joe, for goodness sake!" she chastened. "Why on earth would you say such a thing?"

Aunt Margaret resounded: "Oh, my word, Joe, we thought you would be pleased! You need to think of someone other than yourself, you know." Aunt Leela and Aunt Lucia said nothing.

Mama motioned for all the sisters to leave, told me with her eyes to wait beside Daddy, then hastened directly to the bathroom where she stayed for hardly more than five minutes. When she emerged, she had brushed and smoothed her hair, rearranged it in its usual, large bun at the nape of her neck, had removed all the jewelry, and had scrubbed away all the makeup. Her face was red, almost raw; and as she came near me and toward Daddy's bed, I saw a lone but very large tear poised and glistening on her right cheek — the evidence of hurt which she quickly wiped away.

She looked at Daddy, touched my shoulder, then hastened behind the screen. When she reappeared, she was wearing a gray dress (from several conservative ones hanging on the rack there behind the screen) and low-heeled gray shoes, but kept the lace handkerchief in her hand.

By this time, the nurse was trying my father's blood pressure (as I had buzzed for her). As she saw my mother reappear, the nurse nodded to her, tilted her head to one side, then shook it unobtrusively to record understanding, empathy.

Mama went to Daddy, who by this time was weeping — something I had never before witnessed. "Oh, Eva — I am so sorry. I didn't mean what I said." My mother said nothing, but reached inside the oxygen tent, took my father's hand and kissed it, and held it to her cheek. Daddy sobbed. Mama rubbed his shoulder, wiped his tears, while murmuring softly to him words I could not understand, words that I had no need to understand. Soon, Daddy was quiet; and Mama turned to me, and with her eyes, told me to leave for a while. I obeyed as a matter of course, but felt relieved to be away from all this — something I felt unable to handle, or to comprehend.

For a full month thereafter, my mother spoke to no one in the family except my father — not even to me, although I (her baby) often tried to engage her in conversation. She would touch me on the cheek, the arm, the shoulder — in motherly understanding; but she would not talk. Neither would she smile.

All the apologies in the world would never heal the wound that my father had inflicted, although my mother never mentioned the occasion. Understandably, or not so understandably, my mother's sisters did not often visit my father thereafter.

No one but Mama could love so much, understand so much, endure so much — and forgive so much — and carry on with such great devotion for her husband, my father. Imperfect as he was, Daddy loved Mama with all his heart. No doubt, she loved him more.

It was on an especially momentous visit to the doctor's office, some seven months after the "hospital" incident (I was still just 17), that the physician called me in and conversed privately with me, telling me in no uncertain terms that my father would not live more than two or three weeks at the most, and for me to inform my mother. The electrocardiogram, among other tests, was very "telling." What startling news for the "baby boy" — something apologetically acknowledged even by the doctor while he was advising me.

My immensely discerning father must have surmised the revelation given me, for it was on this return trip home (from the doctor's office) that he made what, to me, was a binding request. "Promise me — when the Lord sees fit to take me — that you will look after your 'mammy' for me after I am gone." (He referred to Mama as our "mammy" when speaking of her thus — in remembrance of the affectionate way in which he referred to his own mother, who had died when he was twelve.)

I assured him that of course I would look after Mama in the event of his death. I had practically sworn that I would protect and "look after" her, but upon reflection, I am well aware that I did not live up to the expectation; and I am sorry. Daddy had loved Mama so.

When young, Joe Ellis had been an avid horseman, a proficient dancer; and was fun-loving, sociable, and just as gregarious as Mama was demure and reserved. Mama often mused (after I became an adult and she felt comfortable to convey such information) that when they attended parties (when courting and then after early marriage), all the young women in attendance stood in line to dance with Daddy.

Mama — prim, quiet, impeccably dressed, ever elegant, and poised — preferred to sit at a table with friends, sip punch or tea, nibble on party treats, and watch the ballroom

activities — accepting only an occasional dance offer from other gentlemen. (Older relatives related these facts to me, when conversing of "how things had been when Eva was young and so beautiful.")

Mama herself preferred the slow music: waltzes and "slow dances" which, even during the early 1900s, could be "free styled" by the leading gentleman. Daddy and Ina Murphy (reputed as the best dancers in the county) exhibited great proficiency in the up-tempoed turkey trot and quick step, in particular. I am told that, at such gatherings and socials, my father would dance every dance — one after the other — never tiring, and that he never lacked for partners.

My sister Priscilla, in phone conversations with me, often expresses regret that I was never able to know our father and mother when they were young (as did she and my other sisters) — "when Daddy had been joyful, active, healthy, and so much fun to be around." I do regret being robbed of that blessing, for ill health was his constant companion from the time I was born.

I remember Daddy specifically as the most honest man I ever knew — and one of the most benevolent. A business associate often enjoyed telling me (and others assembled) that my father kept detailed written ledgers, but that he also "kept his books in his head," and could call forth at a moment's notice any transaction he had ever made, as to time, amount, person, item, and occasion.

I am told by older family members that Daddy, like his mother (whom I did not know), had a photographic memory. I personally can attest to that aspect of his mind, as I saw him demonstrate that remarkable ability on many occasions. He could, for example, read a page from a book and recite it

word for word, and designate the ending word on each line of type! Equally noteworthy was the fact that he could work complicated mathematical equations in his head and achieve the correct result — although he could not always explain how he did so.

He was indeed very kindhearted, as I know of numerous occasions when he "pounded" the poor — buying not only groceries but also clothes, furniture, and other items for them; he paid rent for many who were in need; he made loans of money for which he never asked to be repaid. While he was a practical man who was careful with his funds, he nevertheless demonstrated a beneficence I have yet to see surpassed.

Once, my father and I and a tenant (who drove for Daddy at the time) went to a favorite department store to purchase Daddy a suit. My father asked the worker to go inside with him, and he reluctantly agreed. I was about six years of age and had gone along for the ride, as I often did. I followed them inside the store, although "Uncle Abe," as we children respectfully called the driver-worker, stood back and motioned for me to go in front of him. He stood by the door, ready to exit at a moment's notice.

Inside the store, I witnessed something that, during this era (the mid-1940s), appeared quite strange to all present. When the clerk who usually waited on Daddy came to assist him, my father asked him to fit Uncle Abe instead.

Uncle Abe, though accustomed to my father's kind gestures, expressed some disbelief and nervousness, but accepted my father's generosity with gratitude. Uncle Abe needed a suit for a special family occasion, but could not afford to buy one. So, my father, through this action, showed again the attitude of caring and giving that marked his character

so nobly. He did not, to my knowledge, ever allow Uncle Abe to repay him.

Ironically, this man, my father, who expressed immense kindness to everyone he knew, did not always appear as understanding and accepting of me as I thought appropriate. That is to say, while he appreciated and encouraged my artistic endeavors, my love of music and all the arts — especially my drawing and painting — he nevertheless became impatient with me when I could not express myself, nor perform, in more practical ways.

He wanted me to be adept in "the ways of the farm": physical toil, labor; using farm equipment and implements with ease, "hooking up team" (farm animals: mules, horses); constructing: building, sawing, nailing, framing the side of a barn; or repairing a tobacco truck.

When I failed miserably in these attempts, he could not hide his disappointment nor always hold his anger. He also expressed some obvious frustration (and embarrassment) that I could not "sit" a horse well, nor handle the ponies and saddle horse he bought for me and tried to teach me to ride.

He crushed my soul one day when he said in disgust, after I had done something (in his sight) "just as wrong as it possibly could be done": "You can't do a blamed thing right!" My father never cursed; the word "blamed" was the nearest he ever got to saying "damned."

On this particular occasion, he sent me home from the field with a slap across the back. He later explained that he was not feeling particularly well and had not meant to be so short-tempered. But his observation regarding my "doing it wrong" was correct. Later, to my good fortune and to his good pleasure, I did learn to do a few farm chores to his satisfaction — but never equal to the expertise of my brothers.

My father astonished me in many ways when I was a child, but one curious aspect of his person fascinated me perhaps more than all others: his ability to use both hands with equal ease. So ambidextrous was he that, without thinking about what he was doing, he would pick up a tool and start "working away" with the hand that was closer to the job.

He would, for example, sometimes hammer nails with his right hand, saw wood with his left, and then switch hands at will, while wiping his brow with the shirtsleeve of the free arm. He invariably scripted his rather fancy penmanship with his right hand, but combed his hair with his left; and when necessary (though seldom did he practice the art), he would discipline with the hand nearer the subject. My son, Nathan, and his young son, both manifest a measure of this ambidextrous skill; and so do I, but to a lesser degree.

Regrettably, it was suggested by one person in Mama's family that it was my father who took her violin and "sold it to a traveling man" for only a few dollars, shortly after he and my mother were married — "for tobacco seed."

Whether there was any truth in that accusation, I cannot know — but I sincerely doubt it. I find it difficult to imagine that anyone would dare blame my father this way. I do not believe that he would have taken from my mother something to which she attached such sentimental value: a gift from her father, an instrument she loved to play. It did not conform to my father's character to do anything like that.

I prefer to believe what one of my father's relatives told: that Daddy was having the ancient instrument restrung for Mama; and the man doing the job, perhaps recognizing the value of the violin, fled with it, never to return. The "few dollars" seen changing hands was payment for an unusual tobacco pipe the traveling man had admired of Daddy's: one of several in my father's collection with which he thought he could part. I do not believe my father would have sold my mother's violin for any amount of money!

The most honest of men, he would not, could not, intentionally violate his strict code of principles. Above all, he would never intentionally have hurt my mother — and if so, only out of utter desperation.

I regret that I did not appreciate all that there was to be admired about Daddy until he died. I am glad that he was my father, but am sorry that Divine Providence did not permit me to "keep" him longer — and to understand him better.

•On my most recent visit back home to Bayden, North Carolina, I explored the old dwelling that held so much splendor for me in my youth and young adulthood: Mama's home (where also Daddy had resided). Sadly, because it has remained empty, unlived-in, since December of 1985 — and along with the effects of windstorms, snow and rain; neglect, natural decay, breaking and entering, and perhaps a degree of disinterest, though not intentional abuse — the old house has deteriorated almost to the point of "falling down."

I cannot adequately explain how deeply I am affected by the sight of its decay, as I always associate the old place with my father and mother and the wonders that they and the house represented for my siblings and me. It is also a place of historical significance to the Confederacy, as cited earlier in the story.

Rebecca Ann accompanied me when I visited the old place in late 2003. Observing my very obvious, emotional reaction, she said to me in a comforting way (knowing my sentimentality): "I suppose those of us who pass by so often are not affected quite the same way you are — maybe we have gotten too used to seeing it this way. But I know how you feel."

She swallowed hard as she finished her words. There were tears in her eyes, too.

The porch on which Mama so often sat "during peaceful twilights" was still almost intact — or, at least the major portion of it was.

And sitting there so poignantly amid the ruins was Mama's green rocker: paint peeling, joints loose; no doubt tossed and turned, tortured by wind and rain, assaulted by whatever came near, by whatever could or would assail.

Sitting there so poignantly amid the ruins of my mother's home — still on the porch — was Mama's green rocker: tossed and turned, tortured by wind and rain, assaulted by whatever came near, by whatever could or would assail. I touched it gently — in much the same way I had touched her coffin during that last moment at the grave. Emotion welled up within me. I had been rocked in that chair as a child . . . during peaceful twilights.

I went up to the rocker, touched it gently — in much the same way I had touched her coffin during that last moment with her at the grave. I felt welling up inside me the self-same emotion I had felt then, and that which I feel even as I write these words.

The rocker, minus its seat and back cushions, sat empty — literally, and symbolically so. Paradoxically, it was also occupied — filled with memories: pain and sorrow; dread and discontent; and, at the same time, joy, comfort, security, tranquility, rest. *Rest?* My mind, not my heart, chose that word.

I asked my sister if she might save the rocker for me: the rocker that had sat on that porch since 1985 — and so many years previous to that time. She said yes. By phone, I asked permission of the family member who owns the old place, and she told me that she understood and appreciated why I might want the chair, and that she had no objection. Her voice choked with emotion, too, as she answered me. Why she, or someone in the family, had not removed the chair, I am not certain; but I think I have some idea.

It is strange to me that, during all my visits back home since 1985, I personally had not asked that the chair be removed and saved. I cannot explain, except to say that perhaps I thought it belonged right where it had been for so many years: undisturbed except by natural elements. It was (and is), after all, a fixed part of the past: of Mama and of what she was in a metaphorical sense — a sort of permanency for me and for the others; but in particular for me, since I was and am the youngest. One has to be the "baby" in a family of siblings to understand fully what I mean by that statement. I had been rocked in that chair as a child.

Rebecca Ann asked me if I should like the chair professionally refinished and glued, and fashioned with a new seat, so that it might be used again. I told her that I would think on that and get back to her with my decision, knowing most assuredly that (for whatever reason) I wanted it to remain just as it was: with all the scars of the years. It well matches my heart.

•A word about Brandy, Mama's loving, white German shepherd: Brandy would be found by the groundskeeper at Bayden Cemetery, lying at the foot of Mama's grave a few days after her interment, it was told. How he knew that particular grave was that of his mistress, no one could explain or understand. When discovered, Brandy was said to

Mama's loving, white German shepherd (shown here circa1983 during happier days) would be found by the groundskeeper at Bayden Cemetery, lying at the foot of Mama's grave a few days after her interment — and was said to make periodic visits to the gravesite for as long as he lived. Dear, sweet Brandy loved Mama for as long as he had breath.

be lying prone with his head between his paws, in the exact position he had chosen when he had lain beside her bed while Mama was so critically ill. He seemed oblivious to the presence of any who came near the grave. I am told that he made periodic visits to the gravesite for as long as he lived. Dear, sweet Brandywyne von Ellis, who loved Mama for as long as he had breath. "When all others forsake, . . ."

•After my mother was buried, Tammy, the old tabby cat who shared the company of Mama and Brandy on the porch — and who "answered" Mama as though she understood every word she said to her — would go away from home and never return. It was as if she already knew what I, all these years, have had such a hard time understanding — as Thomas Wolfe, a fellow North Carolinian, suggested: "One really *cannot* go home again. . . ."

•It is logical for one to wonder why, under the weight of the immense grief described in the story which I sincerely experienced, I was nevertheless able to observe details of attire, settings, and circumstances. My main explanation is that noticing in a critical and intense manner has been a trait of mine since childhood.

Indeed, I was taught to note details, even to record (mentally or tangibly, when possible) elements particularly important to me but that might not impress others. I therefore documented specific occurrences as they unfolded — sometimes mentally, sometimes in writing.

No doubt, my "powers" of observation and my mental ability to record and retain facts are inborn: an adjunct to my artistic leaning, or perhaps a carryover from my father's photographic memory. I know that I observe intricate components of things and events which others might ignore or find uninteresting, but I am glad to have that trait. Moreover, because I have a good memory, I am able to call forth remembrances as needed, even when doing so is painful for me.

•Another specific question, among many, might come to the reader's mind: "Why have you waited so long to publish an account of true events that happened nineteen years ago — in 1985 — and which have weighed so heavily on your consciousness?"

There are many reasons that I delayed, but perhaps most significant is that the total story was not quite ready — although the manuscript had been reviewed and accepted for publication by three companies, and had sparked some interest from a major publisher.

So much more has happened since 1985 that, in the evolution of time, I believe the additional information needed to be included. Whether my delay thereto was directed by a force outside myself, I cannot say. I only know that some pressing issues required some address — and perhaps redress.

During a recent phone conversation, a former classmate of mine (knowing something of the guilt with which I still view myself) stressed in firm tones: "Sonny — Sonny — why can't you just let it *go*? There are some things *worse* than *death*, you know." I realize how true that is, but I have yet to be able to "just let it go." *Perhaps someday . . . when the wounded heart has healed.*

I conclude with those simple, spontaneous words that came involuntarily so many years ago from my inner self: words that both puzzled and startled my nephew William the night we were leaving the funeral home — words that

sum up here all that I have attempted to convey — words that at once haunt me but console me more than all others:

"Sleep softly, Mama."

That reflection — that peaceful exhortation — I express in tender thought, as I did nineteen years ago. I shall hold that commendation in gentle reserve, well knowing that, beyond my control, another, foreboding injunction: "Just let me die" is bound to surface whenever it chooses —

. . . and of its own accord.

END